HOW TO
MAKE
CUT FLOWERS
LAST

HOW TO MAKE CUT FLOWERS LAST

VICTORIA R. KASPERSKI

WILLIAM MORROW & COMPANY, INC.
NEW YORK, 1975

IN MEMORY OF MY FATHER

Contents

~~~~~~

Editor's Foreword

~~~~~~

Flowers in the home, flowers at the altar, flowers on the speaker's table—these are a pleasant aspect of living today. But how chagrined we are if a few hours, or perhaps only one, after our careful work is finished, we are confronted by broken-necked Roses, desperately-dying Dahlias, shattered Phlox, or shriveled Daffodils—sad dilemmas, all of which can be avoided. Because at Barrows we have long been aware of this special problem of arrangers, we welcomed Victoria R. Kasperski's careful discussion of the whole subject of making plant materials last after they are cut. In this book she covers the extensive scientific research on the subject, and also gives her own invaluable practical methods. Worked out during her six years' experience as Arranger at Mount Vernon, they cover a wide range of types and make it possible now for us to enjoy our favorite cut flowers over a period of days—or even weeks. We are happy to present so helpful a book, and one so much needed by all who love flowers and want them to last.

HELEN VAN PELT WILSON

How It Happened

THIS BOOK is first of all the result of my own curiosity. For six years, it has been my work—and my pleasure—to arrange flowers and foliages to grace the handsome old house where George and Martha Washington once lived. The gardens here offered a great variety of plant material and, for the most part, an abundance of it. Since a great many bouquets were needed, and these both in winter, when flowers are always scarce, and in summer, when heat and drought check blooming here as elsewhere, it was important to me to have arrangements stay presentable as long as possible. I often asked myself, while gathering baskets of Roses or annuals, or judiciously selecting sprays of berried Holly, just what makes some things last so well, others, despite my best efforts, scarcely pull through one fresh day.

For the answers I sought out all available printed information on the subject, the result of considerable scientific inquiry carried on both in this country and abroad. Further experimentation revealed various ways and means of life-extension which had not been noted elsewhere. Then friends interested in keeping flowers fresh in their homes or for their church services, and also my students in arranging who were concerned with flower-show exhibits, constantly queried me on methods and techniques which would make flowers and foliages, and decorative fruits and vegetables last for a really satisfactory period.

This book is the result. Here is a resumé of what I have discovered myself or learned from others. I hope the information contained herein encourages you to make cut flowers a part of your daily life and helps you to derive added days of pleasure from them. I have indicated under each plant material what I consider to be a sensible expectation of presentability provided it is fresh and of good quality to start with and placed under fairly ideal conditions. For instance, when I say Bachelors-Buttons last 5 to 8 days, I do not mean that *all* the flowers will stay fresh that long, rather that the bouquet will be useful for that number of days. Although all the flowers may not survive the whole period, some of them certainly will. Those that keep well can be put into smaller arrangements or rearranged perhaps to suit the shortened stems. Convictions on what constitutes a "useful fresh flower" vary.

All who are interested in this subject seem as eager to share their discoveries as they are to gain new knowledge. Many enthusiasts have contributed to this book. In addition to many friends—both professional and amateur gardeners—special thanks are due to:

My publishers, M. Barrows & Company, Inc. Working with their staff has been a wonderful and rewarding experience. Helen Van Pelt Wilson has been most generous with ideas and has shared her own knowledge of the subject. This book has grown under her direction. Thanks are indeed due to Margaret C. Lancaster, Garden Consultant, of Washington, D. C., for suggesting Barrows to me.

Charles F. Garner and Mr. & Mrs. F. W. Ballard

of Newport News, and Mr. & Mrs. H. G. Williams of Warwick, Virginia. They have generously shared their valuable information on Roses, fruitful results of experiments over a period of years.

Charles A. Mendez, Jr. for the interest and diligence with which he worked on the preliminary illustrations.

Mrs. McCook Knox for her inspiration and helpful suggestions regarding the manuscript.

Mrs. Edward L. Alexander, Miss Miriam Camp, Mrs. Clifton H. Luce, and Mrs. Sydney L. Manson, Jr., for their eager approval of the idea of this book and their encouragement toward bringing it to completion.

Mr. & Mrs. Gustavus Tuckerman for aid in the technical side of manuscript preparation.

The Mount Vernon Ladies' Association for the privilege of working with such a variety of flowers, of watching them grow to maturity, and cutting them from the lovely gardens for bouquets to beautify the home of the General and his Lady.

VICTORIA R. KASPERSKI

Mount Vernon
Virginia

I

To Make Them Last

~~~~~~

An arrangement is only as good as its condition—on this we are all agreed. And condition depends on the care with which flowers and foliage are cut and handled before they are displayed. "Conditioning" and "hardening-off" are terms applied to this prior treatment which usually involves placing stems in a vessel of cold water and letting them remain there overnight in a cool, dark room.

Plants vary in structure and lasting qualities. Each has its own peculiarities and needs. We should know these in order to give the most beneficial treatment. Specific suggestions for conditioning some 300 plant materials are given in this book. Often it is recognition of some small idiosyncrasy that makes the difference between flowers that last and flowers that fade. Thus the Mockorange has a longer life when much of the foliage is removed from the branch, but the Chrysanthemum needs foliage for long survival.

Methods of cultivation in greenhouse or home garden greatly affect the lasting quality of plants. Actually it is not the number of flowers gathered from one plant that is most rewarding, but the number of days the cut flowers last. Soil fertility plays an important part in producing quality flowers which do not readily shed their petals. Excessive feeding, especially with nitrogen, may lead to large, soft growth with flowers and foliage that are easily damaged. They look beautiful, but are short-lived.

Too much or too little water during the growing period, temperatures that are too high or too low, over-forcing, perhaps inadequate shading—these are factors which adversely affect keeping quality. Indeed you need not always blame yourself if your cut flowers do not last: it may be they were not grown under conditions to make them good keepers. We have all had the experience, I think, of having handsome greenhouse Roses pass on the second day, of buying on a city street, Tulips that did not survive the night.

How Flowers Obtain Moisture

The stem is the lifeline of the flower, and stems vary in structure. (A typical stem is shown in Plate 1.) Stems are soft or herbaceous on plants which develop little woody tissue, and tough and hard on shrubs and trees. The majority of annuals, biennials, and perennials have soft stems, as the Delphinium, Foxglove, Larkspur, Lupine, Peony, Petunia, Snapdragon, and Zinnia. Lilacs, Mockoranges, and most shrubs, also plants like the Perennial Chrysanthemum develop hard, woody growth, but the Annual Chrysanthemum is soft and succulent. So we split the stems of the perennial type and condition them in hot water to open up the cells, but we recut the stems of Annual Chrysanthemums under water and then condition them in cold water. In each case, *it is the structure which dictates the treatment.*

Two things happen when stems are cut: the water-conducting vessels are severed, and the adjacent cells are crushed or cut so that the sugar and mineral salts which they contain escape into the water of the container. These substances then promote growth of the ever-present bacteria, and, if an arrangement is placed in a warm room, this growth is accelerated. Slimy substances soon collect around the stem-ends, and the water-conducting vessels are gradually closed. Moisture is no longer freely drawn up. It is, therefore, essential to focus our attention on these two things—stem-ends and water-condition.

The conducting tubes in the stem can be likened to straws in a soda. If the straws are *pinched* at the base, no soda can be drawn up. If stems are *clogged* at the base, no water goes up the stem, and flowers die prematurely.

Cutting Stems Under Water

Cutting stems under water is often recommended, although certain well-controlled experiments would seem to indicate that the practice is ineffective. And it *is* for many types of plant material. In my work at Mt. Vernon, however, I found it useful for certain flowers. If they did not last much longer, at least they had a fresher appearance and better substance while they were presentable. My experiences have been guided by experiments in England reported in the *Journal* of the Royal Horticultural Society. Here is how it works:

When stems are cut *above* water, air bubbles immediately rush into the open cells of the tiny, narrow, moisture-conducting vessels, and the bubbles impede the flow of water up the stems. Cutting stems under water prevents the formation of these air bubbles. However—and this is important—if stems *are* cut under water they should remain under water—and be conditioned in the same water in which they were cut. If stems cut under water are lifted and placed in another container or handled much while they are being arranged, air bubbles may again develop and block the conducting cells.

Let faucet water stand 5 to 10 minutes before use so air bubbles can escape before you place stems in it. If you do not make a practice of carrying a container of water to the garden (and I urge you to do this), fill the conditioning containers with water before you go out to gather flowers. By the time you return with the cut material, the air bubbles will have vanished.

These are the flowers definitely benefited by recutting under water: Annual Chrysanthemums, Asters, Boston Yellow Daisies or Marguerites, Carnations, Marigolds, Snapdragons, and Sweet Peas. (More are indicated in the alphabetical list.) Calendulas and Stock have been treated in this way with *no* appreciable difference in keeping quality.

Conditioning in the Dark

Why do we condition flowers in a darkened room? On the underside of leaves there are numerous minute pores or stomata, sometimes referred to as guard or breathing cells. These pores open and close to regulate the amount of, and the rate of, carbon dioxide absorption, the liberation of oxygen, and the loss of moisture. At night, when it is dark, these breathing cells almost close. This reduces the amount and rate of moisture-loss, although some transpiration goes on of course. In the daytime, if the room for conditioning is darkened, these stomata, which normally would be open, tend to close, thus decreasing moisture evaporation through the breathing cells of the foliage.

When to Cut

There are two opinions, and votes are cast for both early evening and morning. Following advice from Pennsylvania State College, I have long made it a practice to gather flowers late in the afternoon after the sun has gone down or during the very last hours of daylight. Plants build up a food-supply through sunny hours. So, at the end of the day, food-content in bloom and stem is at the peak. This maximum food-content helps to prolong life after flowers are cut. Furthermore, the end of the day is usually the more *convenient* time. If cut in the morning, plant material is all too likely to remain in the conditioning containers until next morning, when there is time to arrange it. In some cases, this doesn't matter, but for most material the overnight 8 hours of conditioning suffice.

The second best time to gather flowers is very early in the morning before the sun is high and the dew has dried on the petals. If you interpret "cut in the morning" as any time before noon, you will not have good results. Only very early cutting, especially in hot weather, will do.

Compare either time with cutting at midday, after the sun has for hours drawn moisture from the plants. At that time there is an initial loss from which the cut flower has difficulty recovering.

As I have said, it's a fine idea to carry a container of water to the garden. Then you can place stems in water as fast as you cut them. If this is impossible, on your way in from the garden, stop at the nearest water-outlet and drench the cut stems. This is especially helpful when evening or very early morning proves inconvenient to your busy schedule and you must pick during the heat of the day.

Unless otherwise suggested, flowers should be gathered in the advanced-bud or nearly-mature stage. If cut at the tight-bud stage, many flowers are so soft they will not keep well, nor will they continue to open. On the other hand, if cut after they have completely matured or passed their prime, their life will be short. The ability to stay alive and fresh after being cut is a varying characteristic. Boston Yellow Daisies, Carnations, and Chrysanthemums can be expected to last for days, even weeks. In some cases, as with Passion-Flowers, Southern Magnolias, and Water-lilies, we can do little to prolong life beyond 1 or 2 days.

How to Cut

Cut stems *slantwise* with a sharp knife rather than a scissors. All soft stems *must* be cut with a knife. Use sharp pruning shears or a small saw for heavy branches. The *slanting* cut has a number of advantages over the straight-across cut. First it benefits the plant from which material is being removed. A slanting cut, especially on a rose-bush or other plant with stems or branches of some size, heals faster. It collects less moisture than the straight cut. Nor can a slant-cut stem come to rest flat on the bottom of a container, seal over, and so possibly be cut off from the water supply. The slanting cut does not squeeze the stem-cells as the straight cut inclines to do. And if you must split stems, it is easier to work with the slanting cut. Finally, more cells are exposed for water-

Plate 1

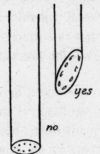

Slanting cut increases
water-conducting surface.

yes

no

To avoid squeezing tubes,
use a sharp knife
rather than a scissors.

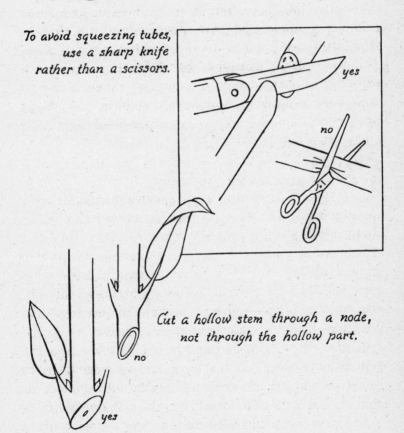

yes

no

Cut a hollow stem through a node,
not through the hollow part.

no

yes

intake. It has been *proved* that Azaleas, Currants, Hawthorns, and Lilacs, as well as Roses, are on this account particularly benefited. Definitely, I have had more lasting results when I cut their stems on the slant and then split them. (See Plate 1.)

For the benefit of the cut flower, the best place to cut the stem is just *below* a node, that swelling on the stem where leaf or leaf-stem joins the main stem. However, for the benefit of the plant which remains, the best place to cut is just *above* a node. This practice encourages plants to branch out gracefully. You can accomplish both purposes with ease if you cut just *above* nodes when removing stems from plants, and recut just *below* the nodes prior to conditioning. (See page 145.)

Cut with discrimination. Keep in mind the beauty and health of the whole plant. Cutting toward outside buds and breaks results in more attractive growth.

Many small annuals and perennials last longest when entire plants are lifted with roots attached to do the job of water-conduction. Clarkia, English Daisies, Godetia, Heliophila, Nemesia, Pansies, and Sweet Alyssum are just a few benefited by this method.

Depth of Water

Is deep water essential for conditioning? Do flowers keep better in tall vases than in shallow tray-type containers? Does long-stemmed foliage have a longer life than short-stemmed? These are important queries. Tests made by the Horticultural Department at Ohio State University show that, with few exceptions (Carnations for one), almost all water absorbed by cut flowers enters through the base of the stem. So shallow water is as good as deep water *so far as intake is concerned*. But in the initial conditioning of cut flowers it is also important to protect them against *loss* of moisture through petals, foliage and stems. This is best accomplished by using generous amounts of water—especially if the atmosphere is very dry. Therefore, when we condition in deep water or submerge plant material, our purpose is to reduce evaporation. Deep water is most beneficial for Cyclamens, Hyacinths, and Calla Lilies, which have leafless stems. Incidentally, experiments indicate that flowers with long stems have no brighter future than those with short stems.

Aids to Conditioning

Handle flowers quickly, by their stems. Delicate and fragile blossoms, like those of the Basket-Flower, Camellia, Gardenia, and Southern Magnolia, may be permanently damaged if you brush one against another or carelessly place them in basket or container.

Handle flowers as little as possible. Lay them down with great care. Cultivate the habit of placing them on tables and work surfaces so heads extend over the edge. Better still, when arranging, lift flowers by the stems and place directly from the conditioning container into the vase or bowl.

Change the water frequently to prevent high concentrations of bacteria. Although this is a simple enough procedure, it is most effective in prolonging the life of flowers. Even when preservatives—commercial or homemade—are added, I find it is best to change water after 2 days and to prepare a fresh solution at that time.

Take care also to maintain a water-level high enough to keep the stem-ends always in water. Water soon evaporates from shallow containers placed in warm rooms. It must often be replenished. It's a good idea at night to lift out such arrangements, pinholder and all, and place in deeper water until morning. Or you can place the whole shallow container inside another larger and deeper vessel of water for overnight. This is not for the purpose of increasing areas of water-intake, of course, but to reduce evaporation from stems and leaves.

Set containers in a cool, dark room for at least 8 hours, preferably overnight. Some material needs 24 hours, as Artemesias and their foliage, Boston Daisies, and Nasturtium leaves. (*Details are given under each material in the alphabetical list.*)

Avoid a close atmosphere. There should be a free circulation of air where flowers are being conditioned, but place containers away from drafts. Also avoid exposure to sunlight and nearness to heating pipes and radiators.

It's a big help if you condition plant material where humidity is high. Try to duplicate the conditions of a greenhouse. Do this with an atomizer, a mist-sprayer, or some similar apparatus. (I use a bottle-type spray with a plastic fixture that won't rust. I bought it at a service station where such sprayers are used to clean windshields.) Spray a fine mist of cold water into the air above and around flowers and foliage after you have placed them with stems in water. A thin film of moisture will settle on petals and foliage and thus increase humidity in a room and prevent undue loss of moisture through flowers and leaves.

Factors That Prolong Life

Since a high proportion of the weight of freshly-cut flowers is water—from 75 to 90 per cent, depending on variety—it is essential to make available to them artificially a copious amount of moisture directly after they are cut. There are not many exceptions to this immediate need. Only a few flowers, like Gladiolus and Marigold, respond well to slight wilting and actually benefit by being left out of water for a time after they are cut. (The alphabetical list includes a few more.) Keep in mind too that there is a point in the wilting of flowers from which recovery is no longer possible and permanent fading takes place.

Here are some suggestions for checking the development of bacteria in water and the subsequent clogging of water-conducting vessels in stems:

Keep conditioning containers, vases, etc. absolutely clean. After each use, wash with hot sudsy water, to which a little ammonia has been added.

Add certain chemicals to the water, as suggested below.

Remove choked ends of stems by cutting and recutting. The clean, new surface thus presented again opens up the conducting vessels which can then take up a maximum amount of water. This is most effective when done early; recutting stems for the first time after the fifth or sixth day is too late.

When milky or colorless juices flow out freely from cut stems, as from Poinsettias, Poppies, or Oleander, dip stem-ends into boiling water. This seals the cells from which the sticky substances flow, and so prevents clogging. In addition, it tends to expand the adjacent water-conducting structures. True, boiling water kills some stem-tissue and so, to a degree, encourges bacterial growth, but this is the lesser of two evils.

Reduce the leaf-surface by removing foliage unnecessary for decoration. This checks transpiration or water evaporation and so noticeably prolongs the life of *some* cut flowers. Lilacs, Mockoranges, Zinnias, and the very large-flowered Dahlias are so benefited, but others, like Chrysanthemums and Pansies are not helped.

Remove all foliage from the area of stem which extends below the water-line in the container unless you are using a sturdy foliage, as that of Rose or Carnation for pattern and design in a glass container. Such leaves are thick enough to remain in water for some time without deteriorating. You cannot do this with foliage of Snapdragons and Dahlias which, when submerged, decays in a matter of hours.

Avoid using soft greenery or cut-up fern in containers as a holding medium. It decays quickly, makes water odorous. When something other than a pinholder is required, I prefer chicken wire, Oasis, Snowpak, crushed Styrofoam, vermiculite, or a device of split twigs lodged in the opening of the container.

Remove the outer or under row of petals from double flowers, like Chrysanthemums, Dahlias, Peonies, and Roses if these are wilted or injured. Flowers then appear fresh again. (This is also a good way to reduce the size of a flower when smaller blooms are needed.)

To prevent curling of large leaves or shattering of petals of dried flowers, use one of the plastic sprays but only on *backs* of petals or undersides of leaves. Clear, colored, silver or gold, they are obtainable from florist or hardware store. They come in press-button cans and so are very easy to apply. (Spray-O-Namel, which I have used, is manufactured by Illinois Bronze Powder Co., Chicago, Ill.)

How to Keep Corsages

Treat your corsage kindly and it will look fresh for more than one wearing. After the first time, remove ribbons and submerge flowers (except Orchids and Sweet Peas) in cold water for 15 to 30 minutes. When petals are crisp, lift out and shake off surplus water. Cover lightly with moistened cotton or shredded paper and wrap loosely in aluminum foil, pinching edges together to seal package. Or place in the original covered box or wrapping. Store in the section of the refrigerator where the temperature is above freezing. For Orchids or Sweet Peas, place with stems in cold water in a container which supports blooms above water. Store in the least-cold location in the refrigerator, preferably at about 50° F.

Chemicals to Prolong Life

Various chemical formulas have been developed which, added to water, check the growth of bacteria and so aid in keeping flowers fresh. They are available under various trade names, as Aladdin, Bloomlife, Floralife, and Survival 77. Generally sold at florists' shops or florist-supply houses, they can also be purchased at most hardware stores. (Addresses of manufacturers are given on page 186.)

We also know that the addition of sugar or salt beneficially affects the metabolism of cut flowers—sugar as a nutrient, and salt to help some flowers absorb water, as Begonias and Coreopsis.

Our old friend, aspirin, it seems has no value.

Keep the pennies in your purse! Copper so added has no value for cut material.

Besides checking the growth of bacteria, certain chemicals, correctly used, will keep flowers from opening too fast, cause more florets to open, prevent early petal-drop, strengthen stems, and delay fading of color in petals and foliage.

A simple home-formula will lower the pH of water where this is necessary. Just add 3 heaping teaspoons of sugar and 2 tablespoons of white distilled vinegar to each quart of water. This is sufficient to lower pH from 7 to 4, and so provide ideal conditions for many flowers, notably Carnations, Larkspur, Roses, Snapdragons, Stock, and others.

Determining the pH of faucet water is simple when you have the proper indicator. The Central Scientific Company (1700 Irving Park Road, Chicago 13) manufactures for the purpose a Hydrion paper which comes in a handy dispenser. With it, you can easily check your water supply, and then adjust it to the pH desired. (At Mt. Vernon I sometimes used spring-water testing about pH 4, and for this no special treatment was necessary.)

About Charcoal

And now a word about charcoal. Broken or chunk charcoal is obtainable from fuel companies, hardware, and garden-supply stores.

Because of its porous structure, charcoal offers a very large surface. This makes it useful as an absorbent. It is phenomenally effective in removing offensive odors from water and also undesirable coloring matter. A few chunks placed in the container for all-green or other long-lasting arrangements help keep water sweet. Before you use charcoal rinse it in cold water to remove soot or loose particles that would cloud the water.

Factors That Hasten Fading

Flowers which have been visited by insects and flowers whose pollen has ripened and been dispersed soon drop their petals. The natural cycle has been completed. The blossom has served its purpose and will now continue maturing toward the formation of seed, the period of ovulation. Once pollination has been accomplished, fading is inevitable.

The presence of ethylene gas hastens deterioration. During the decaying process of petals and leaves of cut materials, minute amounts escape. Traces may also be found where quantities of flowers are improperly stored—as in commercial establishments lacking up-to-date facilities. The importance of a fresh atmosphere for cut flowers is further emphasized by this information.

High heat and low humidity are other adverse factors. The temperature and humidity of the room in which flowers are placed almost wholly determine the rate of transpiration. As the room temperature rises, a greater quantity of water escapes through petals and leaves. Extreme heat causes more water to escape than can be conducted up the stem for replacement. A simple procedure like placing flowers in a cool spot overnight helps them recuperate and makes them last longer. Even placing bouquets on the floor at night, where it is naturally cooler unless you have radiant heat, or placing them in a cooler room at night may add days of life.

To illustrate the affect of temperature on the lasting qualities of flowers, I give here the results of tests reported in the *Journal* of the Royal Horticultural Society. Allowing for the fact that some flowers *naturally* last longer than others, it was determined that cut flowers indoors will often last:

3 weeks in a temperature of 50° F.

5 to 6 days in a temperature of 60° to 65° F.

2 to 3 days in a temperature of 70° F.

I have already mentioned the value of a humid atmosphere and have suggested the use of a sprayer to obtain it.

Values and Dangers of Refrigeration

If short-stemmed flowers are to be used for corsages or gifts, and an ice (not electric) refrigerator is available, place flowers in it in a container of water. The melting ice supplies beneficial humidity. In ice refrigerators the temperatures will not be too low. Insert short-stemmed flowers (Gardenias, Camellias, Hibiscus) in a bed of wet cotton placed in a box of sufficient depth, as a shoe box, to hold the flowers. With Gardenias and Camellias, put on the cover to keep flowers from turning brown.

Gas or electric *home* refrigerators may be used providing there is plenty of room and the temperature is not too low. If it is below 50° F., it may do more harm than good. True, a low temperature may keep flowers in good condition while they are refrigerated but maturing is hastened when they are subsequently brought to room temperatures of 68° to 75° F. Furthermore, flowers generally do not react favorably to sudden changes in temperature, and home mechanical refrigerators usually operate at a low humidity. This is also detrimental to cut flowers.

Florists' large walk-in refrigerators, which are mechanically operated, are a different matter. They may be kept as low as 40° F. but in these, air is constantly circulated to prevent damage to blooms. In *dry-pack* commercial storehouses temperatures may go as low as 31° F., but then flowers are not stored with stems in water. They are sealed in a package that is almost a vacuum. There is almost no air to draw moisture from flowers and leaves and so they remain in an "arrested stage of development" until removed.

It has been determined that refrigeration is not beneficial to all cut flowers. A *Journal* of the Royal Horticultural Society reports: "Flowers of Gladiolus and Coreopsis kept cool and then subjected to higher temperatures did not last long, the former only a few hours. . . . [In the case of Wedgwood Iris,] freshly cut buds lasted, in water, for 4 days at 70° F., or if cut at maturity, for only 3 days, but after 1 week's dry cold storage at 32° or 40° the keeping quality was reduced to one day at 70° F. . . ." (Sudden transference from cold storage to rooms of 70° F. or thereabouts is highly unnatural.)

Concerning Containers

The most satisfactory containers for conditioning are of glass, pottery, wood, agate, or other material which will not rust. (Galvanized tin is not good, especially when preservatives are used.)

Containers should be roomy. Avoid narrow-necked types for conditioning: they tend to squeeze the stems.

Always use *clean water* and *clean containers*. Again, may I urge you to wash containers after each use with plenty of hot sudsy water to which a little ammonia has been added. Then you can be sure no lingering bacteria will remain from the last bouquet.

II

Special Treatment for Special Groups

~~~~~~~~~~~~~~~~~~~~~~~~~~~~~~~~~~~~

Woody Branches

EXAMPLES: Crab-Apple, Flowering Quince, Forsythia, Lilac, Mockorange, Perennial Chrysanthemums.

Split stem-ends for 3 to 4 inches. (With short branches, 1 to 2 inches is enough.) Remove leaves and flowers from portion of branch which will extend below the water-line in the conditioning container. Cut woody flowering material while partially in bud. Give required conditioning period. Crushing ends of branches with a hammer has long been recommended. Splitting is far better. Crushed ends may take up moisture, to be sure, but particles of damaged tissue foul the water and promote bacterial growth, which soon clogs stems. (See also, Forcing Flowering Branches.)

Stems with Milky, Yellow, or Colorless Fluid

EXAMPLES: Some Campanulas, Oleander, Poinsettias, Poppies.

Here are two possible treatments. Steep 1 to 2 inches of the stem-ends in boiling water for 1½ to 3 minutes while protecting upper leaves and flower-heads from rising steam. One way to do this is to push ends of stems through 2 or 3 thicknesses of newspaper. Gently fold the protective paper up and around foliage and flowers in cornucopia fashion, leaving base of stems accessible to the boiling water.

Or split stems for an inch or more and sear in a flame. A convenient way to do this is to light a candle and place it in a holder or in a glass tumbler. Hold end of each stem directly in the flame for about 15 seconds, or while you count to 15 slowly. (See Plate 5.) Sear stems to the *full length* that will be required in the finished arrangement. If it is necessary to recut stems at any time, the new cut must again be seared.

Searing or exposure to boiling water does not eliminate the need for conditioning. Treated stems should immediately be placed in water for the required time so that the water-conducting apparatus can go into action. A *Journal* of the Royal Horticultural Society explains it this way:

"On cutting of some plants . . . latex (a milky juice in some plants yielding rubber) exudes, which on solidifying, chokes the wood vessels (which are next to the vessels containing latex) and prevents much uptake of water. Stems may be split (for 1 or 2 inches) to aid dispersion of latex and present a larger surface for water uptake. *Or* these lactiferous tubes may be closed by heat [boiling water or searing with a flame]. The dispersion of latex from some plants may be so slow as to be almost unnoticeable. This is especially true of Malvaceous plants." (Among these are Hibiscus, Hollyhock, and Swamp Rose-Mallow.)

Hollow Stems

EXAMPLES: Some Campanulas, some Dahlias, also Hollyhocks.

Place stems in hot water, 100° F. Let remain until water cools. Then add cold water to bring water-level higher in container. Hot water quickly damages foliage, so don't let it reach leaves important to the arrangement you plan. Water should not be steaming. If it is, chances are that it is hotter than 100° F. (Not all flowers with hollow stems require this treatment. See alphabetical list.)

Herbaceous Woody Stems

EXAMPLES: Some Chrysanthemums, Lantana, Stock.

Split ends of stems and place in hot water, 100° F. Let flowers remain overnight in the cooled water. (Prematurely wilted flowers can often be revived by this treatment.)

Bulbs

EXAMPLES: Hyacinths, Scillas, Tulips.

Cut stems diagonally with a very sharp knife. Remove thick white portion at base of each stem—unless this is needed to give height to an arrangement. In that case, split stem up through the white portion into the green. Condition with stems in cold water. When cutting bulbs from your garden, spare most of the foliage. Its function, after flowers have bloomed, is to manufacture food in the bulb for next year's flowers. (See various bulbs in alphabetical list for specific treatment.)

Hairy Stems

EXAMPLES: Calendulas, some Geraniums, Heliotrope.
Place stems in quite hot water, 80° to 100°
F. Let remain for required conditioning period.

FLOWERS FOR THE SHOW

In the judging of artistic arrangements or of specimen blossoms, "Condition of Material" is always considered and allowed a certain number of points in scoring. To win a blue ribbon, material must be at its most beautiful stage of development and well conditioned at the time of exhibiting.

The transportation of cut flowers to a show presents various problems. Time and effort are wasted if, upon arrival, flowers are wilted, crushed, or bruised. Here are a few common-sense suggestions which you will find helpful.

First of all condition properly as suggested for each kind in the alphabetical list.

During transit, avoid drafts, extremes of heat and cold, and crowding.

When packing flowers, follow the commercial method. You will need sturdy cardboard boxes, newspapers, and plenty of florist's thin wax paper. Pack with great care. Put only as many flowers in each box as will fit without crowding.

For a short journey, line boxes with wax paper, letting part of the large sheets hang over the sides. After flowers are placed, fold the extra paper over the flowers so that a cover-within-a-cover results. This double protection of paper and box conserves moisture and creates humidity. (See Plate 2.)

For long distances, line the wax paper with a second layer of wet, but not dripping, newspaper.

In very cold weather, better obtain a commercial liner and fit it into the box or insulate with several thicknesses of dry newspaper, before any wax paper, as a precaution against freezing.

Aluminum foil and moisture- and vaporproof plastic materials make more effective linings than thin wax paper. They keep moisture in, cold or heat out. One exhibitor, transporting flowers via automobile on a broiling-hot day from Baltimore to Boston, used a plastic with such success that the blossoms arrived with dewy-fresh petals. Other exhibitors were amazed at the excellent condition of what proved to be prize-winning material after travel over such a distance.

If stems are long—that is, too long for the box—cut out one end of the box and fold this back. Stems can then extend through the opening. A visit to your florist will reveal other easy but helpful techniques of packing.

Place the more fragile flowers and the fully-opened blossoms on separate cushions of crumbled wax paper to keep them apart and prevent crushing against each other and against the sides and bottom of the box.

Arrange so that some flower-heads are at one end of box, some at the other, the stems dovetailing in the center.

Lay a sheet of thin wax paper or a single sheet of wet, but not dripping, newspaper between layers of flowers. The damp newspaper increases humidity. Or you can lightly spray each layer of flowers with a very fine mist of cold water to keep them fresh. But do not spray Orchids, Sweet Peas, Calla Lilies, Bearded Iris, or similar delicate blooms for they will spot.

Flowers can be transported with stems in water. Metal

Plate 2

Line box with
wax paper.

Dovetail stems
in center.

Avoid
overcrowding.

Separate layers with
damp newspaper.

Fold over excess
wax paper. Cover.

Support fragile flowers
on crushed wax paper.

containers, made especially for this purpose, are now available. They are designed like a pair of pails, a tall, convenient handle in the middle. Inexpensive, they can be found in garden-supply shops. For traveling, put a few stones in the bottom of each section to prevent tipping, and place a stick or reed in the center of each bunch to prevent downward pressure of wrapping material. Let the stick or reed be a few inches higher than the tallest bloom. Then wrap flower-heads—plus the reed—loosely, but securely, with wax paper or some plastic material as protection against wind and sun en route. Fill containers with water and put in the wrapped bunches.

These double containers also make perfect workroom accessories for conditioning flowers or for holding indispensable greens. Or fill with water and take them to the garden to receive flowers as you cut them.

A finished arrangement can be transported easily only if there is someone to hold it in transit. Otherwise place it in a suitable box with bricks or stone placed against the container to steady it. And you must cover such supports with newspaper or cloth so they won't damage vase or bowl. A packing of crushed newspaper around the container also helps. Wrap the top of the arrangement loosely with thin wax paper to guard against drafts.

Flowers for the Church

To have lasting arrangements in church, first select flowers that are naturally enduring. All these do well: Amaryllis, Asters, Azaleas, Carnations, Celosia, Chrysanthemums, Dahlias, Daisies, Delphinium, Hydrangea, Gladiolus, Iris (other than the Bearded), Larkspur, Lilacs, Lilies (Calla, Easter, Madonna, Rubrum), Magnolia (but not *Magnolia grandiflora,* unless lasting qualities are not important), Marigolds, Narcissus, Peonies, Phlox, Rhododendron, Roses, Snapdragons, Stock, Tuberoses, and Zinnias. Forced fruit branches and many flowering and foliage shrubs and trees are also excellent.

Condition well before arranging. Of course be sure containers are clean. A commercial preservative is well worth using with flowers for the church unless containers are made of metal. Usually manufacturers recommend their preparations be used in "other than metal containers." So you should guard against injury to cherished, and sometimes irreplaceable, church vases.

Arrange the night before or early in the morning of the service. Store in a *cool* room free from drafts and away from sunlight.

Spray flowers that can take it with a fine mist of cold water after they are arranged.

Just before final placement in church or chapel, check the water-level in the containers, making sure that they are completely filled and that all stems reach down into water.

To more or less permanent evergreen arrangements, add a few chunks of charcoal. And change the water weekly. If you use a preservative, water need not be changed so frequently, but check to be sure it does not all evaporate.

Adjust the pH of the water to suit individual needs. This is well worth while. (See alphabetical list.)

After service, remove flowers to a cool place. If the church vases are narrow-necked, as they usually are, you may have to remove flowers from the crowded containers and recondition them. This will often hold them beyond your expectations.

In air-conditioned churches and those cooled by large

electric fans, try to place flowers out of direct air currents. Since this is sometimes impossible, let arrangements stay in place just for the service. Then remove them to more agreeable locations so as to prolong their life.

Flowers from Your Florist

Unpack flowers as soon as you receive them. Examine stem-ends, flower-heads, and foliage for freshness. If stems appear black or coated over, recut with a sharp knife, removing ½ to 1 inch, depending on length of stem and extent of damage.

Remove any bruised leaves and petals.

Recondition 2 to 3 hours before arranging to allow flowers to regain any moisture lost while in transit. It is possible flowers were packed hours before delivery to your door.

Florists' flowers always have had a conditioning period. You need only carry on where professional care was interrupted.

Useful Equipment

Plenty of water
Cool dark room
Adequate containers (some for
    submerging)
Sharp knife
Scissors with long, thin blades
Sharp pruning shears
Small saw for cutting branches too large
    for shears
Candle with holder and matches

Wax: paraffin or candle ends (in colors to match flowers)

Facilities for boiling water and melting wax

Hydrion paper to determine pH of water

Syringe or Windex-type sprayer

Stiff brushes, soap, and ammonia

Soft brush for removing pollen from exhibition flowers

Long-necked watering can or pitcher

Orchid tubes

Cotton for cleansing large leaves

Plastic spray

Clear shellac

Twistems

Newspapers

Wrapping material: aluminum foil, plastic sheets, plastic bags, florist's thin wax paper

Commercial mailers and liners

Cellulose sponge for clean-up

Special Aids

Alcohol, rubbing (drugstore)

Alum, powdered (drugstore)

Aluminum Sulphate (garden-supply house)

Borax, powdered (drugstore)

Calcium Nitrate (garden-supply house)

Charcoal (fuel company, hardware store)

Glycerin (drugstore)

Oil of peppermint (drugstore)

Preservatives, commercial (florist, hardware store)

Salt
Sugar
Sylpho Napthol for gourds (drugstore)
Vinegar (distilled white)

III

"Keeping" Directions:
Acacia to Zinnia

~~~~~~

ACACIA OR MIMOSA (*Acacia Farnesiana, A. dealbata*)

Lasts 1 to 1½ weeks. Cut branches when they are half in flower, half in bud. Split at base. Condition overnight in cold water. With Acacia from the florist, recut and split stems and condition at least 4 hours before arranging. To insure fragrance, wrap blossoms in cellophane or wax paper until you are ready to arrange them. The humidity created inside the wrapping also keeps flowers fresh, and encourages buds to unfold. In Europe, a variety with silvery leaves, *A. dealbata*, is forced into flower in November—well ahead of the normal spring season. Stems are placed in water in a dark, warm shed and the budded branches subjected to steam. These European-grown Acacias appear in our flower shops early in spring. They are flown here immediately after being cut.

Acer (See Maple)
Achillea (See Yarrow)
Aconitum (See Monkshood)

ADAMS-NEEDLE (*Yucca filamentosa*)

Lasts 4 to 7 days. Few settings are large enough for the entire flowering stems of Yucca, but you can easily use side blooms or side shoots cut from the main stem at the advanced-bud stage. Split stems and condition overnight in about 6 inches of cold water. If you wish, you can open the great white buds. Submerge them in a large container of cold water and gently turn back the petals. Let flowers remain under water until petals are crisp; then lift out and place stems in cold water until you are ready to arrange.

AFRICAN VIOLETS (*Saintpaulia ionantha*)

Cut only newly-opened flowers and they will last a week; those that have been open for several days soon fade. Stems are soft and damage easily so use a sharp knife or snip off at the base with a long, thin scissors. Recut stems under water and condition overnight in warm water to start with.

Emily Stuebing of Pittsburgh has worked out a good method of keeping African Violets from shattering:

"I cut off the flowers and, with the faces down on waxed paper, carefully brush the back of each petal where it touches the calix with egg-white and water—about half and half. The egg-white should not be beaten but just mixed with the water by stirring. The egg-white can be applied with a little cotton on a toothpick or a tiny brush; a cleaned nail-polish brush will do. In a short time the blossoms will be dry and there is no need to worry about petals falling off. Need I caution exhibitors that this egg-white must not show? Of course it would not be applied to flowers in specimen classes."

Foliage is seldom used in arranging but it lasts well and actually shows roots in a short time. Condition leaves overnight in warm water to start with.

AGAPANTHUS OR LILY-OF-THE-NILE
(*Agapanthus umbellatus*)

Lasts up to 7 days. Cut when the outer rim of the flower cluster is showing its funnels. Buds open *after* they are cut. Condition stems overnight in cold water and let remain until flower clusters are somewhat open.

Ageratum (See Floss-Flower)

ALKANET OR SUMMER FORGET-ME-NOT
(*Anchusa italica*)

Florets continue to open for about 10 days. This is most desirable for cutting because of its unusual, vivid-blue color. Set plants close together in the border. As they begin to blossom, thin by pulling out plants with roots attached. Otherwise, it is difficult to get long stems unless plants are quite large. Cut the central stems first; plants will then branch out and go on blooming. Wash away soil from roots and condition overnight with cold water to start with. Arrange in opaque containers.

Allium (See Yorktown Onion)
Aloysia citriodora (See Lemon-Verbena)
Alstroemeria (See Peruvian Lily)

ALTHEA OR ROSE-OF-SHARON
(*Hibiscus syriacus*)

Florets last about 2 days; buds continue to open over a 7-day period. Cut branches with one open flower and several buds ready to unfold. (Very tight buds will not open in water, but they still make excellent decoration.) Split woody stems. Spray foliage and buds with a fine mist of cold water. Place stems in cold water overnight, or until buds unfold. Allow ample room in container for unfolding of flowers. Remove faded flowers as fresh buds open. Condition *foliage* or non-flowering branches for at least 24 hours.

Althea rosea (See Hollyhock)
Alyssum maritimum (See Sweet Alyssum)
Alyssum saxatile (See Basket-of-Gold)
Amaranthus caudatus (See Love-Lies-Bleeding)

AMARYLLIS (*Hippeastrum Reginae*)

Flowers last 4 to 7 days, buds a day or so longer. Cut flowers in opening-bud stage or immediately after one or two have completely opened on the stalk. (Let foliage remain on plant so food can be manufactured in the bulb for the following season.) Split flower-stems and condition overnight in cold water to which 1 tablespoon of ammonia has been added for each 2 quarts of water. This checks growth of bacteria. If conditioned beforehand, Amaryllis also last remarkably well when arranged without water. If foliage is used, condition overnight in 4 to 5 inches of cold water.

AMARYLLIS, SUMMER (*Lycoris radiata*)

Florets last 2 to 3 days; buds go on opening 4 to 8 days. Cut when flower clusters are half open. Split stems. Condition overnight in cold water. Recut stems if they decay at base. Remove faded flowers from clusters as buds continue to open.

AMAZON- OR EUCHARIS-LILY
(*Eucharis grandiflora*)

Lasts up to 6 days. Available at florists from Christmas until Easter. Used primarily for corsages, but fine for low arrangements, especially when water-area is featured. Insert the short stems in wet cotton. Store in covered box in refrigerator (with temperature *above* freezing). Or, split stems for an inch or so and condition overnight with stems in cold water. When arranging, place flowers so petals do not touch water, but rest above it. Flowers deteriorate rapidly if saturated with water. Well-conditioned, they hold up for a week. When combining with fruit, place stems in orchid tubes or fasten moist cotton to ends with a wrap of waterproof tape.

Amelanchier canadensis (See Shadbush)
Ananas sativus (See Pineapple)
Anchusa italica (See Alkanet)
Andromeda (See Pieris)

ANEMONE OR WIND-FLOWER (*Anemone* in variety)

Lasts 7 to 12 days. Cut when petals are wide open, but while centers are still tight. Or cut when large buds freely show color and are ready to burst into flower. Remove lower leaves and place stems loosely in cold water. Let remain overnight. If container is roomy, stems will assume attractive curves. Anemones last at least a week, sometimes longer. Recut stems as necessary to remove the small portion that gets soft or decayed. The Japanese Anemone blooms in gardens from September until late frost. *Anemone coronaria*, the greenhouse variety, is available at florists during late winter and early spring.

ANGELS-TRUMPET (*Datura Meteloides*)

Charming in bud, blossom, and fruit. Flowers last as long as 5 days, but close each night. Cut in advanced-bud stage, that is, when buds are elongated, and petals show true color and are ready to unfold. (If picked full blown, flowers wilt fast and will not recover.) Cut in late afternoon; then buds will open by morning. Avoid touching open flowers or the delicate buds; handle by stems only. Submerge foliage for half an hour before conditioning with stems in cold water. Use seed pods in dried arrangements, with fresh flowers, or in all-green foliage bouquets.

Annual Poinsettia (See Mexican Fire-Plant)
Anthemis (See Golden Marguerite)

ANTHURIUM (*Anthurium* in variety)

Flowers can be kept fresh a month. Cut when fully open, but before pollen on spadix has developed. Split stems. Condition overnight in cold water. If you get these from the florist, recut stems and condition for at least 4 hours, preferably overnight, before arranging. The normally straight, stiff stems may be gently bent with warm hands into graceful curves.

Antirrhinum majus (See Snapdragon)

APPLE BLOSSOMS (*Malus* in variety)

These will last a week or more if branches are cut when buds are well developed and ready to burst, with perhaps one or two fully-opened blossoms. Split woody stems. Place in cold water. Spray with a fine mist of cold water to provide beneficial humidity and help buds open. Branches may be cut in late January or early February and forced into flower. This way you can enjoy the blossoms indoors before the snow has left the branches outdoors. (See Forcing Flowering Branches.)

Armeria maritima (See Sea-Pink)

ARTEMESIA OR WORMWOOD
(*Artemesia* in variety)

Fresh flowers and foliage last 5 to 10 days; dried, their life is indefinite. Cut flowers when only half the spike is open. Cut foliage when the true leaves have developed. Split woody stems. Condition both flowers and foliage for at least 24 hours in deep cold water, stripping leaves from lower stems. If foliage wilts and does not respond to cold water, recut stems, place in hot water, 80° to 100° F., and leaves will soon become turgid and crisp. In this genus are many fine foliages—gray, gray-green, silvery-gray, light- and dark-green—also some excellent flowers for cutting. (See also Dusty Miller.)

Asclepias syriaca (See Milkweed)
Asclepias tuberosa (See Butterfly-Weed)
Asparagus Fern (See Fern, Asparagus)
Aspidistra lurida (See Cast-Iron Plant)

ARTICHOKE (*Cynara Scolymus*)

Keeps up to a month before noticeable shriveling, and is attractive in vegetable and fruit arrangements. Recut the short, thick stem and submerge the whole in cold water for about 1 hour. You can coat with clear shellac, plastic spray, silver or gold paint, and have Artichokes last almost indefinitely.

The big, purple, thistle-like blossom, conditioned overnight in cold water, is distinctive for large-scale *fresh* arrangements and lasts 5 to 7 days. Flowers also dry well, retaining most of their color. When left on plants, they turn a lovely tan. For drying, gather blooms when fully open. Hang to dry in the usual manner, or let flowers go to seed stage and then collect them. (These will be tan.)

ASTER, CHINA (*Callistephus chinensis*)

This can be made to last up to 2 weeks. Cut flowers when three-quarters to fully open. Prepare a sugar solution, using 1 teaspoon of sugar to 1 quart of water. Recut stems under this solution. Let stems remain in it overnight. Foliage of Asters wilts before flowers. Remove leaves from upper stems *only* after they have wilted. Then substitute other appropriate foliage, as flowers will last for several more days. Revive prematurely wilted Asters by placing stems in hot, 80° to 100° F., water.

ASTER, HARDY, OR MICHAELMAS
DAISY (*Aster* in variety)

Lasts 6 to 10 days. Cut when three-quarters of the florets in each cluster are open. Treat the same as China Aster. If stems are woody, split before conditioning.

ASTILBE (*Astilbe* in variety)

Lasts up to 7 days. For fresh arrangements, cut when panicles are half open. Split stems. Condition overnight with stems in cold water. For drying, gather when all the flowers are open or only a few buds remain at tips of panicles. Dries well, retaining color and form, and will not shatter if cut at the proper stage. (Often mistaken for Spirea.)

AUCUBA (*Aucuba japonica*)

Foliage lasts for months and finally roots in water. (There is a variety of this called Gold-Dust Tree with yellow-spotted leaves.) Cut foliage at any time of year. Split woody stems. Condition overnight in water, warm at the start. If you cut in winter, submerge in cold water for 1 to 2 hours to give a crisp, clean look. Then condition as above.

AUTUMN-CROCUS (*Colchicum autumnale*)

Treat cut flowers of lifted bulbs in the same way as the true Crocus which blooms in spring (see Crocus). These are fine for cutting, lasting 3 to 5 days.

AZALEA (*Rhododendron* or *Azalea* in variety)

High humidity is essential for cut Azaleas, and with it they will last 5 to 10 days while buds continue to open. Cut when 3 or 4 florets are completely open on each stem or in each cluster. Buds open well in water. Split woody stems. Condition overnight in cold water. Spray foliage and flowers with a fine mist of cold water to provide humidity, help buds open, and prevent moisture loss through petals. (It does not harm your shrubs to cut blossoms, but try to prune and shape plants as you cut.)

BABYS-BREATH (*Gypsophila* in variety)

Lasts up to 1 week. Cut sprays when half in flower. Condition stems in cold water overnight. Avoid wetting flower petals. You can also dry this for winter bouquets. The double perennial form is best; white varieties may be dyed before or after drying. (See How to Dye Flowers.)

BACHELORS-BUTTON OR CORNFLOWER (*Centaurea Cyanus*)

Lasts 5 to 8 days. Cut flowers when fully open or nearly so. Tight buds, even half-open buds, will not develop afterwards. Cut stems just below a node (swelling on stem). Condition overnight with stems in cold water. Flowers hold petals tenaciously. They may turn a few shades paler after several days in water, but are nonetheless beautiful.

Balloon-Flower (See Chinese Balloon-Flower)

BALSAM OR LADY-SLIPPER (*Impatiens Balsamina*)

Lasts 5 to 6 days. A gem for cutting! Cut when one-half, or slightly fewer, flowers are fully open along the stem. Buds continue to open in water, and stems stretch noticeably. Remove lower florets as they fade. Some of the dwarf, double varieties have a central blossom atop a rosette of leaves. Cut this type immediately after the tip blossom is fully open. Split stems. Remove some foliage from stems of taller sorts to show flowers to better advantage and make them last longer. Condition overnight with stems in cold water. Tall stems will curve gracefully if placed slantwise in container during conditioning. Seed pods are decorative; defoliate and use with fresh or dried materials. If seed pods and stems are soft and green when gathered, condition overnight with stems in cold water before arranging.

BAMBOO (*Bambusa* in variety)

Lasts 1 to 2 weeks. Cut this attractive tropical foliage when it has attained the size and color you want. Condition by submerging in cold water until it is crisp. Lift up but leave stems in cold water till convenient to arrange.

Prepare bamboo *canes* in this way (see Plate 3). Cut sections of canes from plants. Remove the first or top unit just below a node. Fill this hollow top section with water. In lower sections, drill small holes through the sides just below each node. Fill these hollow sections with water also. Cut off the base of the stalks evenly across so they will stand firm. Canes will leaf out, and the fresh green foliage will last for several months, and may be used over and over again.

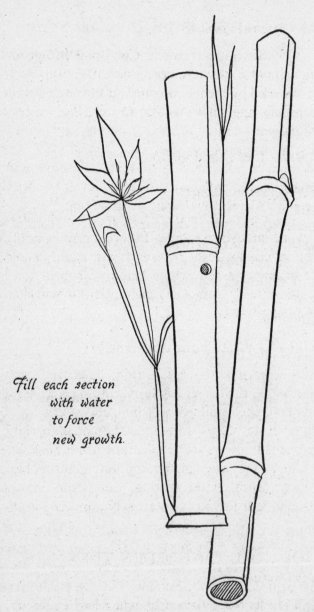

Fill each section
with water
to force
new growth.

Plate 3

BANANA (*Musa abyssinica*)

Lasts up to 1 week. Condition foliage by submerging in cold water until crisp; thereafter keep stems in water until used. When you trim and cut large leaves into smaller sizes, apply lemon juice to cut edges to prevent discoloration.

Baptisia australis (See False Indigo)

BARLEY (*Hordeum vulgare*)

Lasts 1 to 2 weeks. Cut at any stage after stems are strong enough to support flower- or grain-heads. For fresh bouquets, condition overnight with stems in cold water. For drying, cut as ripening begins. Hang in usual manner. Gild or paint for holiday decoration. It will then last almost indefinitely.

BASKET-FLOWER (*Centaurea americana*)

Lasts up to 1 week; tight buds stay fresh longer and may be used again. A flower to discover with luscious colors of shell-pink, clear-white, and delicate lavender. Cut at various stages—fully open, half open, in tight bud. Fully-opened flowers are fragile; they bruise at slightest mishandling. Even when gently laid in the cutting basket, they may crush. After cutting, split stems immediately, place in warm water to start with, and condition overnight.

BASKET-OF-GOLD OR GOLDEN-TUFT
(*Alyssum saxatile*)

Lasts for 5 days. Cut when half in flower. Place stems loosely in cold water overnight. Avoid crowding or crushing. The lovely pale-yellow variety is *citrinum*.

BEARD-TONGUE (*Penstemon* in variety)

Lasts up to 1 week. Cut when one-fourth the flowering stalk has opened. Split stems. Let stems remain in cold water until flowers are sufficiently open—at least overnight. Beautiful, curving stems sometimes occur on plants; curves can be developed by placing stems slantwise in container during conditioning.

BEE-BALM OR OSWEGO-TEA (*Monarda didyma*)

Flowers last 5 to 7 days; buds and foliage to 10 days. Cut when one-quarter of the blooms on each stem are about half open. The others will open nicely in water. Remove about half the leaves. Condition overnight, using warm water to start with.

BEECH (*Fagus* in variety)

Lasts up to 1 month. Budded branches, green-foliaged branches, or golden and bronze autumn leaves—all stages are excellent. Choose branches with interesting curves and perfect leaves. (Remember you are pruning when you cut.) Split woody stems. Condition overnight in warm water to start with.

Beech leaves are handsome when treated with glycerin and water. You do it this way: Select branches of desired length with well-developed leaves early in summer before they are damaged by insects or drought. If foliage is dusty, wash under a spray of cold water. Remove side branches at base, leaving 6 to 10 inches of stem. Split 2 to 3 inches. Place split stems in a solution of 2 parts water to 1 part glycerin. Set container in a dim, dust-free room. Let remain for 2 to 3 weeks, or until foliage has become golden-bronze. (The longer branches remain in solution, the darker leaves become.) When leaves are well colored, remove and store (out of water). The same branches may be used year after year.

Beech leaves can also be pressed. Cut the most vivid branches in fall. Trim away overlapping side growth. Then lay each branch between several thicknesses of newspaper. Weight with boards or heavy books. It takes 3 to 4 weeks (sometimes longer, depending on humidity and climate) for foliage to dry sufficiently. When well dried, remove branches immediately so moisture absorbed by newspapers does not seep back into foliage and cause mildew. Store pressed branches in boxes to keep clean until used.

BEGONIA (*Begonia* in variety)

Short-stemmed flowers of most types and also long sprays of hanging tuberous-rooted Begonias last 4 to 7 days when cut. Foliage lasts a week or more, the sturdier types rooting in water. Cut foliage after it has attained size and color desired. Cut blossoms when clusters are half open. With tuberous-rooted Begonias, cut when fully open unless buds are wanted. Well-developed buds open nicely in water, but blooms are small. Split stems of both foliage and flowers. Condition in large container of cold water to which 1 tablespoon of salt has been added for each 1 quart of water. Avoid breaking the brittle stems. Spray large, decorative leaves of Begonia on the underside *only* with a clear plastic spray to prevent curling.

In *Tuberous Begonias* by Worth Brown this advice is given: "Since moisture is absorbed through the petals, the surface of the flowers should be moistened. This is the method generally recommended by florists: Lay the blossom in the palm of the hand and lower it into a container of clean water until submerged, bring it to the surface, turn it over, and let the excess water run out. Do not shake it. The water which remains down in the base of the petals will keep the flowers fresh for a long time. Some florists prefer to use a fine spray or syringe on the blossoms, but then a lengthy spraying is necessary."

Belamcanda chinensis (See Blackberry-Lily)
Bellis perennis (See English Daisy)

BELLS-OF-IRELAND OR SHELL-FLOWER
  (*Molucella laevis*)

Lasts 1 to 2 weeks. Cut when stems have reached desired length—tiny florets will be fresh inside the bells at tip of stem; they will have faded and fallen out of the bells lower down. Stems usually grow with curves; if you want them more pronounced, submerge stems in cold water for 1 to 2 hours. Then lift out and condition in cold water overnight. Grown in shade, foliage and bracts are blue-green; in full sun, yellow-green. They dry well. Do not cut until they turn silvery-beige; hang to dry. I find this works better than cutting while green and then attempting to dry.

Benzoin aestivale (See Spice-Bush)

BERRIES IN VARIETY

Last 1 to 4 weeks, depending on type. Many ornamental berries mature in late summer and early fall. They have their prime, or most beautiful stage of development, the same as flowers. Although most often used in dried arrangements, they also are attractive arranged with fresh flowers, foliages, and fruits. For fresh arrangements, when stems will be in water, treat like other woody material: Defoliate judiciously; split stems; condition overnight with stems in cold water.

For dried bouquets, cut branches as soon as berries are fully developed. If berries are a type which drops easily, cover with plastic spray before hanging to dry. (This also prevents shrinking to some degree.) Experience alone helps you to determine the proper stage for gathering. Wait for the best color and form to develop, but be sure to get there before the birds do!

Not all berries or fruits dry satisfactorily. Some, like those of Castor-Bean, Firethorn, Holly, and Viburnum, are pulpy, soft, and watery inside. These will not last well —even when covered with plastic spray or shellac. Berries and fruits that dry best have considerable substance, are firm to the touch, like those of Bittersweet, California Pepper-Berry, Cat-tail, Leopard-Lily, and Teazle.

Bignonia radicans (See Trumpet-Vine)

BIRD-OF-PARADISE-FLOWER (*Strelitzia Reginae*)

Lasts 1 to 2 weeks if conditioned in water brought to pH 4. (See page 24.) Several flowers are borne in a boat-shaped bract which grows horizontally at tip of stem. As each flower fades, remove it and gently lift out the next one from within the enclosure. Cut stems on a slant with a razor-sharp knife. If they are difficult to secure on a large pinholder, cut straight across and split for an inch or so. When split stems separate too much, wrap base with a Twistem to facilitate fastening in holder.

Blossoms dry well even after use in fresh arrangements. If stems are strong, it is not necessary to hang upside-down. Just stand upright in a narrow container without water and place in a dark, dry room. Flowers do not retain their color to perfection, but the less vivid effect is still beautiful.

BITTERSWEET (*Celastrus scandens*)

Lasts for years! Gather when fruits are most brilliant, but before heavy frost, drenching fall rain, and wind. Arrange immediately or store. Spray with clear plastic to prevent shriveling and check dropping of fruits, although this cannot be entirely prevented in very warm, dry rooms. If dried arrangements get dusty, spray sparingly with a fine mist of warm water to cleanse them. Arrangements need not be taken apart to do this. Just place on kitchen drainboard or in a bathtub. Let dry well before replacing.

BLACKBERRY- OR LEOPARD-LILY
(*Belamcanda chinensis*)

Florets last 1 to 2 days, clusters continuing to open for 5 to 7 days. Fruits dry well. Cut when 1 or 2 flowers in each cluster are fully open. Condition overnight with stems in cold water reaching almost to flower-heads. Each flower fades and curls into an interesting twist—in itself decorative—buds continue to open. Seed form is fascinating. Pods are tan. They burst to reveal tenacious, shining, jet-black, jewel-like seeds. Cut green fruits to use with fresh materials or dry for winter bouquets. To dry, gather fruits in late summer and early fall when pods are pale tan and show signs of splitting; hang upside-down.

BLACK-EYED SUSAN (*Rudbeckia hirta*)

Lasts 1 to 2 weeks if you cut stems with a sharp knife, slantwise, when flowers are completely open, centers still tight. Condition overnight with stems in cold water. (Foliage survives this submerging.) In arrangements, foliage may wilt before flowers. You can clip it off and substitute other foliage while you enjoy flowers for several more days.

BLANKET-FLOWER (*Gaillardia grandiflora*)

Lasts 7 to 10 days. Cut blossoms when fully opened or when petals are cup-shaped, centers still tight. Split stems. Remove lower leaves with a sharp knife. Condition overnight in a 5 per cent solution of sugar. (Use 4 teaspoons of sugar to each quart of water.) Foliage is firmly attached. Fruits also are attractive and last well before and after maturing.

BLEEDING-HEART (*Dicentra spectabilis*)

Lasts 4 to 6 days. Sharply cut sprays when about half the flowers are open. Cut with care for bruised stems deteriorate quickly. Split stems. Condition overnight in deep cold water. Recut stems as necessary. Avoid taking very much foliage, especially from young plants; it is needed to produce strong growth next year. Foliage of Meadow-Rue (*Thalictrum*) makes a good substitute.

BLUETS (*Houstonia caerulea*)

Rooted sprays last 3 to 5 days. With a trowel, lift plants when half the flowers are open. Handle clusters from the base, since flower-stems are fragile. Wash soil from roots. Condition overnight with roots in cold water. Or cut individual flower sprays with a sharp scissors, and recut stems with knife before conditioning.

BLUE LACE-FLOWER
(*Didiscus* or *Trachymene caerulea*)

Lasts 7 to 10 days. Cut when a quarter to a half of the flower cluster is still in bud. Condition overnight in cold water reaching almost to flower-heads. Some stems will curve if placed slantwise in a container but partially filled with water.

BLUE LOBELIA (*Lobelia siphilitica*)

Lasts 6 to 10 days. Cut when one-quarter to one-half the flowering spike is open, and remove faded flowers as upper buds unfold. Buds open well in water, sometimes losing a little color which only seems to enhance their beauty. Split stems. Strip away lower leaves. Condition overnight in deep cold water, or condition longer, allowing spikes to open more completely, especially if you have cut them in a very early stage. Well-established plants produce many long-stemmed flowers for cutting.

BLUE LYME GRASS (*Poa* in variety)

Lasts for 1 week. Cut early in the season, and again at later stages of development in order to have a diversity of colors. Tie in small bunches. Hang to dry. Test for readiness by holding stems upright. If they do not droop, they are ready to use or store for later arranging.

Blue Salvia (See Sage)
Bocconia cordata (See Plume-Poppy)
Boston Yellow Daisy (See Marguerite)

BOUGAINVILLEA (*Bougainvillea* in variety)

Lasts up to 8 days. Cut when bracts, which enclose the tiny flowers, are fully developed and brightly colored. Split woody stems. Remove most of the foliage. Submerge stems and flowers in cold water until all parts are papery and crisp; ½ to 1 hour should be long enough. Lift up but keep stems in cold water until arranged.

BOUVARDIA (*Bouvardia Humboldti* or *B.* hybrids)

Lasts 4 to 6 days. Fragrant, gleaming-white Bouvardia may be had from the florist the year round; or grow it in conservatory or cool greenhouse, outdoors if it is hardy in your area. Cut when newly open and remove as many leaves as possible. Condition with stems in cold water overnight. If from florist, recut stems immediately, split, and condition at least 2 hours. Florist's Bouvardia is likely to have very short stems; try to order ahead and ask for longest stems available.

Bowstring-Hemp (See Snake-Plant)
Bridal Wreath (See Spirea)

BRODIAEA (*Brodiaea* in variety)

Florets last 1 to 2 days; clusters go on opening for 1 or 2 days longer. A useful midsummer flower well worth discovering. Lovely in bud and showy when used in quantity. Cut when half the flower cluster is open. Condition overnight with stems in cold water.

BROWALLIA (*Browallia speciosa major*)

Lasts 4 to 7 days. Cut when 1 or 2 of the flowers on each stem are fully open. Condition overnight with stems in cold water. Start cutting the short stems early in season. This causes plants to branch and produce many free-blooming, longer-stemmed side shoots.

Brown-Eyed Susan (See Black-Eyed Susan)
Buddleja Davidi (See Butterfly-Bush)
Burning-Bush (See Gas-Plant)

BUTTERCUP, WILD (*Ranunculus* in variety)

Lasts 2 to 4 days. Wilts upon cutting, but revives quickly when stems are split and placed in hot water, 80° to 100° F. Cut when flowers are partly unfolded or cup-shaped, centers still tight. Foliage is insignificant, so plan to use some other kind.

BUTTERFLY OR LITTLE OWL (*Moraea iridioides*)

Lasts but 1 day. Cut when buds are ready to unfold. Place stems in deep cold water overnight; flowers will be fully open the following day. Not especially valuable for cutting, except that striking color combinations make this a curiosity.

BUTTERFLY-BUSH (*Buddleja Davidi*)

Lasts 5 to 8 days. Cut when at least one-half the flowering spike is open, but before the *flowers that have opened first begin to fade*. Split woody stems. Remove all foliage not necessary for decoration. Place stems in hot water, 80° to 100° F. If panicles are not fresh and turgid by the time water cools, place stems in hot water a second time. It may take two or three changes to hot water before flowers are suitable for arranging. Thorough conditioning is all important if Buddleja is to be rewarding as a cut flower. Spraying foliage and flowers very lightly with cold water encourages buds to open, checks water-loss through petals and foliage.

BUTTERFLY-FLOWER OR POOR-MANS-ORCHID (*Schizanthus pinnatus*)

Lasts 4 to 7 days. Cut when about three-quarters of the flowers are open. Split stems. Condition overnight with stems in cold water. If you cut during very hot, dry weather, cover flowers and foliage with a fine mist of cold water as you set them aside for conditioning.

BUTTERFLY-WEED (*Asclepias tuberosa*)

Lasts 5 to 8 days. Gather when clusters are one-half to three-quarters open. Add 2 tablespoons of sugar to each 1 quart of water used for conditioning. Although of the milkweed family, there is little milky juice in stems, and so it is usually unnecessary to sear stems or treat with hot water. However, if they wilt prematurely, the hot-water treatment will quickly revive them. Often recommended for drying, but flower-heads shrink so much, large quantities are needed to make a showing.

CACTUS (*Cactus* in variety)

Most blooms last but 1 day; sometimes only for a few hours. However, well-developed buds of Prickly-pear (*Opuntia camanchica*) continue to open as old flowers fade and so may give a good display for 4 to 5 days. Condition with stems in water overnight. Sections also last well out of water, and base does not deteriorate as when kept moist. You can hold stem-sections in place with wooden picks. (See also Houseleeks.)

CALADIUM (*Caladium* in variety)

Foliage lasts 5 to 10 days. Cut the decorative leaves with a sharp knife when they have attained size desired. Select stems sturdy enough to support leaves. Split stems. Condition overnight in cold water. If leaves seem overly soft, submerge in cold water for about half an hour, or until crisp, before conditioning. To check loss of moisture and prevent curling, spray underside of leaves (*underside only*) with clear plastic. (See page 22.)

Calceolaria (See Slipperwort)
Calico-Bush (See Laurel)
California-Poppy (See Poppy, California)
Calla Lily (See Lily, Calla)
Callistephus chinensis (See Aster, China)
Calluna in variety (See Heather)
Calycanthus fertilis (See Strawberry Shrub)

CAMASS LILY (*Camassia esculenta*)

Lasts 4 to 8 days as flowers continue opening from the bud stage. Cut when about one-quarter of the flowering spike is open. Split stems. Condition overnight in deep cold water. Lovely curves result if stems are placed slantwise in large container while conditioning.

CAMELLIA (*Camellia* in variety)

Lasts 3 to 8 days, depending on stage of development. Cut when blossoms are partly open, outer petals separated from the bud, and the rest of the petals loose. Handle as little as possible for flowers bruise easily. With thought for next year's buds, cut mostly short stems and plan low arrangements or use in corsages. Insert short stems in a box of wet cotton, spray with a fine mist of cold water, *cover*, and store in a refrigerator at a temperature of 45° to 50° F. overnight, or until you wish to use flowers. This prolongs life and the closed box helps prevent browning of petals. Or you can split stems and condition in shallow containers of cold water overnight in a dark room. Then, before arranging, quickly dip flowers in cold water (avoid soaking) and work with wet hands to prevent injury to petals. Only if Camellias wilt prematurely, try submerging them in cold water to make petals crisp again. Spray Camellia arrangements once a day, covering petals and foliage with a fine mist of cold water. Where plants are hardy and can spare whole branches for arrangements, cut and condition the same as other woody material (page 28).

Campanula Medium (See Canterbury Bells)
Campsis radicans (See Trumpet-Vine)

CANDYTUFT (*Iberis sempervirens* or *umbellata*)

Lasts 5 to 7 days. Cut the hardy *sempervirens* with a section of woody growth when flower clusters are one-quarter to one-half open. Split woody stems and carefully remove close-growing foliage from lower portions which will go under water. Condition overnight in warm water to start with. Cut the annual type, *I. umbellata*, sometimes called Globe Candytuft, when halfway out and condition overnight in cold water.

Canna generalis (See Lily, Canna)

CANTERBURY BELLS (*Campanula Medium*)

Lasts 1 to 2 weeks. For longest life, cut when stalks are one-quarter to one-half open, but for beauty, and better color, though shorter life, cut when nearly full blown. Since stems contain a milky juice, condition in hot water, 100° F., to start with, and let remain overnight. If there is premature wilting, recut stems, split, and sear ends in a flame for 15 seconds; then condition, starting with the hot water. Remove faded flowers as new ones open.

Cape-Jasmine (See Gardenia)

CARDINAL-FLOWER (*Lobelia cardinalis*)

Lasts 5 to 7 days. Cut when one-quarter of flowering stem is open. If cut at a later stage, lower flowers will fade before upper ones open, and effect will be poor. Split stems and sear ends in a flame for 15 seconds. Then place in warm water and let remain overnight.

CARNATION (*Dianthus Caryophyllus*)

One of the most lasting of all cut flowers, often remaining fresh for 10 days. Cut when flowers are three-quarters open and pistils are about the same length as petals. Recut stems, slantwise, under water. Carnations have hard nodes along stems through which it is difficult for water to pass, so condition overnight in cold water reaching right up to the flower-heads. Foliage need not be removed except at base of stems. It does not decay quickly when submerged and leaves help absorb water which eventually finds its way to flowers. After they are arranged, spray with a fine mist of cold water, but do not let them get dripping wet. Commercially, Carnations are kept as long as 30 days. Flowers are allowed to wilt slightly after cutting. Then they are packed in airtight containers, without water, and stored at 33° F. Air outside containers is kept fresh and circulating. Upon removal from storage, stems are recut and conditioned in deep water overnight. Flowers are then ready for market.

Carolina Allspice (See Strawberry Shrub)

CAST-IRON PLANT (*Aspidistra lurida*)

Leaves last for months when cut. Every arranger should have a few Aspidistras as a ready source of green. Cut foliage at point where it joins the plant and take as much stem as possible. First submerge in cold water for about an hour; then place leaves upright in a few inches of cold water overnight or longer. To produce a special line, loop, or curve, roll and tie leaves as you wish and submerge in cold water until the form is set. One to 2 hours is long enough for young, tender foliage—older, tougher leaves take a little longer. Lift and condition with stems in shallow water until arranged. Allow leaves to dry *before* untying and they will retain their new form after being arranged.

CASTOR-BEAN OR CASTOR-OIL-PLANT
(*Ricinus communis*)

Flowers and fruits last up to 10 days after cutting; foliage lasts even longer. This large plant, growing 8 to 9 feet in one season and spreading 4 to 5 feet, produces deeply-cut palmate leaves of varying size and color— green, greenish-red, greenish-bronze to bronze—treasures for the arranger. Fruits look spiny, are first green, then vivid orange to crimson. Flowers are cream. At certain stages of growth, a perfect arrangement can literally be cut in one piece from a plant.

Cut blossoms when about half the spike is in flower. Cut fruits any time after they are formed. Fruits do not dry well; they lose color and substance. Condition flowers and fruits by submerging in cold water for 1 to 1½ hours— until crisp and firm. Lift up but keep stems in cold water until used. Cut foliage when size and desired color are attained. Split stems and condition overnight in warm water to start with.

CAT-TAIL (*Typha latifolia*)

Lasts indefinitely. Gather early in the season, as soon as cat-tails are formed, usually in June or early July. Collected later in the season, they tend to shatter. If you must gather them late, you can check shattering by spraying with clear plastic or dipping in clear shellac immediately after cutting. When so coated, they can be used several seasons. Cat-tails are also attractive painted silver, gold, or a color to harmonize in an arrangement.

Celastrus scandens (See Bittersweet)
Celosia (See Cockscomb)
Centaurea americana (See Basket-Flower)
Centaurea cyanus (See Bachelors-Button)
Centranthus rubra (See Jupiters-Beard)
Cercis canadensis (See Redbud)

CHASTE-TREE (*Vitex Agnus-castus*)

Lasts 5 to 7 days. Prune and shape shrub when cutting material for arranging. Cut flowering spikes when but a few buds are showing color. Flowers last longer when allowed to open indoors. Remove *all* foliage from flowering stalks. Split stems. Condition overnight, in warm water to start with. If foliage is desired, cut some non-flowering branches. Condition similarly. Fruits of Vitex dry well. Gather when green and firm. Hang to dry.

Cheiranthus Cheiri (See Wallflower)

CHERRY BLOSSOMS (*Prunus* in variety)

Flowers last 5 to 15 days as buds continue to open. Cut when only a few buds along the stem have burst. Split woody stems. Condition in cold water overnight, or long enough for a sufficient number of blossoms to open. To hasten opening of buds, place stems in warm or hot water (up to 100° F.) once daily and leave until water cools. Spraying branches once a day with cold water also hastens opening of buds. Double varieties do not open well if cut at the bud stage. With these, wait until about three-quarters of the flowers are open. Then treat as above. (See also Forcing Flowering Branches.)

CHINESE BALLOON- OR BELL-FLOWER
(*Platycodon grandiflora*)

Lasts 5 to 7 days as buds continue to open. Cut when 2 or 3 flowers on each stem are completely open. The large inflated buds will then open in water but not the small tight ones. To check escape of milky juice in stem, split stems and place ends in boiling water for 1 ½ to 3 minutes. *Or* hold end of each split stem in a flame while you count to 15 slowly. Then condition by placing stems in a sugar solution—use 4 teaspoons of sugar to 1 quart of warm water. Let remain overnight.

CHINESE LANTERN-PLANT
(*Physalis Alkekengi* or *P. Bunyardi*)

Gather when fruits are a vivid orange and of papery texture. Split some pods into three or more sections. Cut along the veins from tip to base so pods will curl into interesting shapes. Remove all foliage from stems. Tie in small bunches. Dry upright so that pods will hang gracefully. (See How to Dry Flowers.) When completely dry, spray with clear plastic to preserve pods almost indefinitely. However, they last well without this treatment. Lanterns gathered green tend to shrivel and drop during drying, but they can be used green in fresh or dried arrangements if they are first conditioned overnight with stems in cold water.

CHINESE OR ORNAMENTAL EGGPLANT
(*Solanum integrifolium* or *S. coccineum*)

This lasts almost indefinitely. Gather the scarlet or yellow tomato-like fruits in late summer and early fall when they are fully developed and firm to touch. Do this before severe frost, preferably during a dry spell. Water-soaked fruits soon spoil. Remove all foliage and trim branches to desired lengths. Store in a cold (above freezing) place until used.

Christmas Greens (See Evergreens)

CHRISTMAS OR LENTEN ROSE
(*Helleborus niger, H. orientalis*)

Lasts for weeks. Blooms through early and late winter and right into early spring. Blossoms seem to keep forever when cut, although color fades. Split the stems. Condition overnight in deep cold water. The foliage is evergreen but not good for cutting. Furthermore, unless plants are very well established, they will be stronger each year if foliage is not cut. A good substitute foliage is Pachysandra, which can always be spared.

CHRISTMAS TREES

Keep fresh 3 to 4 weeks if well cared for and in a not-too-hot room. Select a fresh, green tree to begin with. Branches should be soft and pliable, foliage fragrant and of bright color. Feel the cut trunk. If it is moist with sap, the tree is probably fresh cut. Needles turning brown or crisp to touch indicate a tree has already lost much moisture.

If possible, before trimming, keep tree outdoors or in a cold garage. With a saw, cut across the trunk on a slant about 1 inch above the original cut. Set trunk in a pail of water, warm to start with, and sprinkle or spray branches daily with cold water. When you are ready to decorate, try to place your tree in a cool spot, away from radiators, fireplaces, television sets, and other sources of heat. To keep tree fresh, support trunk in a container of moist sand and keep this wet. You can improvise a stand by corking the drainage hole of a large flower-pot, filling this with sand, and then setting the pot in a large waterproof tub.

For safety: Never use lighted candles near or on tree or near other greens that have become dry and crisp. Check electric lights, light connections, and wires. Watch out for frayed wires or loose connections on or near tree. Keep electric toys away from tree; also wrapping paper and other inflammable materials.

CHRYSANTHEMUM (*Chrysanthemum* in variety)

Among the most lasting of cut flowers— from 1 to 3 weeks, or longer. The annual type usually has soft stems. Recut stems under water. Begin the overnight conditioning in cold water to which 3 to 4 level table-spoons of sugar have been added for each quart. For just a few flowers, 3 tablespoons is about right—large quanti-ties of flowers in the same container would require 4 table-spoons. Perennial mums often have hard, woody stems. Split these for 2 to 5 inches, depending on length. Condi-tion in water hot to begin with, 100° F., and with the same amount of sugar. If flowers wilt prematurely, give them the hot-water treatment (see page 30).

Tests at Ohio State University proved that splitting stems was an important factor in prolonging the life of mums. The *Journal* of the Royal Horticultural Society reported that tests indicated mums lasted longer when leaves were left on stems. Of course they can stay for shallow arrangements, but in deep containers, foliage must be stripped off below the water line for it deteriorates rapidly. Since all foliage wilts before flowers, remove it as necessary and substitute other fresh greens; flowers may still last for days.

Mums grown on the West Coast are cut and packed, without being placed in water, and flown across the continent. Upon arrival, stems are recut and placed in hot water. Flowers respond beautifully and are sold in eastern flower shops looking as fresh as though they had just been picked.

Chrysanthemum frutescens (See Marguerite)
Chrysanthemum Parthenium (See Feverfew)

CINERARIA (*Cineraria* hybrids)

Lasts 5 to 7 days. Cut flower clusters when about three-quarters of the florets are open, but before pollen in center is mature. Avoid wetting foliage; it decays rapidly and may also spot. However, foliage is rarely used as cut material. Condition overnight with stems in warm water to begin with. Ask your florist for the double variety. Not as widely grown as the single, it is enchanting.

Cinnamon Fern (See Fern, Cinnamon)
Cirsium (See Thistle)
Cissus rhombifolia (See Grape Ivy)
Citrus (See Orange Blossoms)

CLARKIA (*Clarkia elegans*)

Lasts 5 to 7 days as buds continue to open. Superior for cutting. Lift small plants from the cutting garden or plant them so close together in a border that you can thin them out as they begin to blossom. Condition with roots in water overnight. Or cut stalks just before they are ready to unfold into flower with perhaps 3 or 4 of the lower florets fully open. Split stems. Condition overnight with stems in cold water. Cutting the central flowering spike encourages branching and repeated blooming of plants.

CLEMATIS (*Clematis* in variety)

Lasts 5 to 8 days, depending on variety, if some of the old wood is cut with each spray of bloom. (This is true of most flowering vines.) Cut hybrids when newly opened, or just before petals are ready to unfold. Types blooming in small clusters should be cut when no more than one-quarter is open. Split woody stems. Condition in cold water overnight. Long stems may be shortened after flowers and buds are well supplied with moisture. Place shortened stems in water for a few more hours before arranging.

Cleome spinosa (See Spider-Flower)

CLIVIA (*Clivia* hybrids)

Florets last 2 to 3 days, clusters continuing to open up to 10 days, depending on number of buds. Cut when slightly more than half the cluster is open. If taken at the proper stage, it will be sufficiently developed to continue opening in water. Recut and split stems. Then condition overnight with stems in deep cold water. Recondition Clivia obtained from a florist.

CLOVER (*Trifolium* in variety)

Lasts 5 to 8 days. Cut when flowers are about three-quarters open. Remove foliage not needed for decoration. Condition overnight in cold water. Flowers of pink and red clover retain color, shape, and a delicate "country sweetness" when dried for winter use. For drying, cut when blossoms are fully open. Hang to dry.

COCKSCOMB (*Celosia* in variety)

Lasts 1 to 3 weeks, depending on variety. Plume types, crested and feathery blooms, and silvery spikes delicately tipped rose, also the foliage of some varieties are excellent for fresh bouquets or for drying. Cut plume type when at least three-quarters developed; under-developed flowers do not keep. Remove lowest leaves and others not necessary for decoration. Cut crested types when they are the size and shade of color desired. Cool autumn weather intensifies hues. Condition overnight in cold water. The fine *Celosia plumosa*, called Princess Feather, grows tall and straight, but pleasing curves result when stalks are placed slantwise in the container during conditioning. For drying, cut flowers at their most perfect stage and strip off all foliage. Place stems in cold water and let remain until they become turgid and flowers recover from wilting, about 4 hours. Hang to dry.

Codiaeum variegatum (See Croton)
Colchicum autumnale (See Autumn-Crocus)

COLEUS (*Coleus Blumei* or *C.* hybrids)

This excellent variegated foliage lasts almost indefinitely and after 2 to 3 weeks in water, cuttings develop roots. To insure vivid coloring, grow in full sun; in semi- to moderate shade you get larger leaves and more subtle shades. Frequent cutting keeps plants in bounds and shapes them. Split stems. Condition overnight in cold water.

COLUMBINE (*Aquilegia* hybrids, *A. canadensis*)

Lasts 5 to 7 days. Cut when about two-thirds of the individual flowers on each stem are open. Well-developed buds open in water. Try to condition in a cool temperature, 45° to 50° F., with stems in deep, cold water. Avoid wetting flower petals. Don't cut much foliage from younger plants or you will weaken them for next year. Grow Meadow-Rue (*Thalictrum*) as a source of foliage to use with Columbine.

Convallaria majalis (See Lily-of-the-Valley)

CORAL-BELLS (*Heuchera sanguinea*)

Lasts 5 to 10 days. Cut when half the spray is in flower. Condition overnight with stems in cold water. Recut as necessary, removing any black or deteriorated portions. Buds do not open in water. If curving stems are desired, allow sprays to wilt slightly, then place slantwise in container for conditioning.

COREOPSIS (*Coreopsis tinctoria*)

Lasts 1 to 2 weeks. Cut fully-opened flowers but with tight centers. Condition overnight in cold water reaching almost to flower-heads. Add 1 tablespoon of table salt to each quart of water used. Tests indicate that this flower stored at low temperatures, then brought to a living room, does not last as long as when it is conditioned at normal room temperatures. Cut frequently from plants to encourage blooming.

Cornflower (See Bachelors-Button)
Cornus florida (See Dogwood)

COSMOS (*Cosmos bipinnatus*)

Lasts 5 to 8 days. Select blooms whose petals are widespread, centers very tight. If blossoms have a fluffy, powdery, well-developed center with mature pollen, they will not last well; nor will buds develop after being cut. Cut and discard these to encourage further branching and blooming. Condition stems overnight in cold water reaching almost to flower-heads. Upper foliage will not deteriorate if left in deep water for just one night. Watch out for pollen from fully-developed flowers. It contains moisture and, when it falls, may cut through a wax polish and mar a table.

COTTON (*Gossypium* in variety)

The white, mallow-like blossoms turn pink and last only a matter of hours. The green "bolls" and foliage last very well. Treat as woody material. Split stems and condition overnight in deep cold water. Gather flowers or white bolls just before they are to be arranged, allowing 1 hour for conditioning. When the natural cotton has faded or discolored, fill the bolls with absorbent cotton and close with colorless glue or cement. Plants will not develop cotton in cool climates, but they are nice to grow for foliage alone.

Cowslip (See Virginia Bluebell, also *Primula*)

CRAPE-MYRTLE (*Lagerstroemia indica*)

Lasts up to 1 week. Cut when some buds in cluster begin to show color. Allow them to open indoors. Outdoor flowers are often damaged by wind and insects. Remove all foliage not necessary for decoration and condition stems in deep water, warm at the start. If you should cut branches after many buds have opened, remove most of the foliage and submerge in cold water for 1 to 2 hours, or until petals are crisp. Then lift up sprays, but keep stems in cold water until used.

Crassula (See Jade Plant)

CROCUS, SPRING (*Crocus vernus*)

Lasts 4 to 6 days; longer if bulbs are lifted with blooms. Crocus incline to open wide too quickly so cut in advanced-bud stage when color is showing freely in petals. Condition overnight with stems in cold water. Tight buds open into small flowers and colors fade slightly. When flowers are sufficiently open, drop a little melted paraffin inside the base of the cup to retard dropping of petals. When arranging crocus, allow plenty of room for petals to open wide, and so display the full beauty of the blossom. Often they are lovelier the second day, after flowers have had a generous drink of water and comfortably stretched their stems. You can also lift the flowering bulbs and plant in low containers with other spring things for long-lasting and refreshing living arrangements. Later, bulbs may be replanted.

Crotallaria retusa (See Rattlebox)

CROTON (*Codiaeum variegatum*)

Freshly-cut foliage will last up to 3 weeks. Wash in cold water. Split woody stems, and condition in cold water overnight. Lower foliage need not be removed. You can also make the large individual leaves assume interesting forms. Roll up, tie, and then submerge in cold water for 1 to 2 hours. Lift out and place with stems in water. Do not untie until foliage has dried.

CROWN IMPERIAL (*Fritillaria imperialis*)

Lasts 4 to 7 days, depending on size of cluster. Cut flowers when cluster is about three-quarters open. Split stems. Condition overnight in cold water. Cut no more foliage than is necessary or bulb is weakened. (Blossoms and crushed stems of this *F. imperialis* have a disagreeable odor so avoid them for arrangements. Grow *F. meleagris* instead.)

CUSHION SPURGE
(*Euphorbia epithymoides* or *E. polychroma*)

Flowers last 5 to 8 days. Cut when the cluster is half open. Sear each stem in a flame while you count slowly to 15. Then place in warm water to condition overnight. Or avoid searing and place at once in hot water, 80° to 100° F., and let remain overnight.

CYCLAMEN (*Cyclamen persicum* or *C. indicum*)

Lasts 5 to 8 days. *Pull* fully-opened blossoms and leaves from plant; do not cut them. Grasp each stem where it is attached to the corm, and give a quick, firm yank, freeing it without leaving behind part of the stem. Portions left attached to the corm decay quickly, causing injury to plant, especially if a large number of buds have not yet opened. Recut and split both flower- and leaf-stems. Condition in cold water overnight. If blooms do not look fresh after 1 to 2 hours in water, recut stems and sear in a flame for 15 seconds. Then put in cold water. Well-developed buds showing color will open in water but blooms will be small. Tight buds will not open but still may be cut to add interest to an arrangement.

Cydonia japonica (See Quince, Flowering)
Cynara Scolymus (See Artichoke)
Cytisus scoparius (See Scotch-Broom)

DAFFODILS OR JONQUILS (*Narcissus* in variety)

Can be held up to 2 weeks. To hold open blooms for exhibition, cut and place in an ice refrigerator at about 48° F., or keep in a cool, dark room. Some varieties, cut when buds are bursting their sheaths, will hold as long as 2 weeks. Remove fallen pollen from throat of show flowers with a soft brush. Use it wet to remove dust spots or moisture blemishes. Cut blossoms when they are newly opened, unless it is necessary to take well-developed buds to hold over for exhibition at a show. Open flowers normally last 5 to 8 days, depending on variety. Avoid cutting much foliage if you value your bulbs. Leaves are necessary to nourish next year's crop. Before conditioning, cut off the white portion at base of stems unless length is needed. Then split through it to green part. To check flow of sticky juice, hold cut ends under warm water for a minute or so. Condition overnight with stems in 3 to 4 inches of cold water. If stems are split, water should reach several inches *above* the split.

DAHLIA (*Dahlia pinnata*)

Lasts 5 to 7 days. Methods of culture greatly affect keeping quality. Overfeeding and overwatering contribute to quick fading. The *Journal* of the Royal Horticultural Society reports that cut Dahlias are benefited by being placed in a weak solution—1 part to 1000—of potassium nitrate (drug or garden shop), rather than in clear water. A pinch to a quart of water is about right. Cut just after flowers have fully opened. Take care to remove any leaves likely to go below the water level for Dahlia foliage deteriorates rapidly if submerged. Place stems of small-flowered types in cold water and leave overnight in a dark, cool place. (Dahlias flowering from seed sown the same season are excellent for cutting. In autumn, you can dig up plants of choice colors, store tubers, and set them out again next year.) Prematurely wilted Dahlias revive quickly when stems are recut and placed in water as warm as your hands can stand, and left there until arranged.

When you cut large flowers for exhibition or home decoration, remove below-water foliage and immediately place stems for 1 to 2 hours in cold water. Then remove to a pan containing 2 to 3 inches of boiling water. The heat destroys air pockets and facilitates water uptake. Finally place stems in a deep container of cold water in a cool spot and let remain there overnight.

DANDELION (*Taraxacum officinale*)

Lasts 1 to 3 days. Gather early in the day as blossoms close when the sun sets. In fact, they sometimes close when picked, sometimes remain open for no apparent reason. Stems are hollow. Sear ends in a flame prior to conditioning.

Datura Meteloides (See Angels-Trumpet)
Daucus carota (See Queen-Annes-Lace)

DAYLILY (*Hemerocallis* in variety)

In subdued light and in a fairly-cool place, individual flowers will last 2 days. Select stems with a number of well-developed buds which may continue to open for a week. Refrigerate sprays of day-blooming varieties and they will open at night for your evening party. Otherwise condition overnight with stems in cold water. Next day some buds will have fully opened. Arrange Daylilies informally so that it will not be necessary to rearrange as first blossoms fade.

DELPHINIUM (*Delphinium elata, D.* hybrids)

Lasts 5 to 10 days as buds continue to open. Cut when about half the florets are open. Condition overnight with stems in cold water. For storage, 48° to 53° F. is best. Allow plenty of room for flowers to open and stems to stretch. Florets bruise easily and break off if tangled. To obtain interesting curves, place some stems slantwise in conditioning container. Remove faded florets before they shatter. (See also Larkspur.)

Delphinium Ajacis (See Larkspur)
Dianthus barbatus (See Sweet William)
Dianthus carthusianorum (See Sweet Wivelsfield)
Dianthus Caryophyllus (See Carnation)
Dicentra spectabilis (See Bleeding-Heart)
Dictamnus fraxinella (See Gas-Plant)

Didiscus caerulea (See Blue Lace-Flower)
Dieffenbachia Seguine (See Dumb-Cane)
Digitalis (See Foxglove)
Dipsacus sylvestris (See Teazle)

DOCK OR SORREL (*Rumex* in variety)

Flowers inconspicuous, fruits used in dried arrangements. Gather at various stages of development—light-green in newly-formed fruits; greenish-tan, bronze, and dark-brown in mature fruits. For interest let a little foliage remain at tip of stems when drying. (See also How to Dry Flowers.)

DOGWOOD (*Cornus flórida*)

Flowers last 7 to 10 days; fruits and buds longer. All through the year this lovely tree offers something to the arranger. In spring, flowers; in summer, sturdy foliage; in fall, red berries and colored leaves; in winter, tight, unusual buds. Cut branches (with regard to shapeliness of tree) immediately after bracts open and before pollen develops in the center of the tiny blossoms. Split woody stems. Condition overnight with stems in warm water to start with. Condition foliage and branches of berries and winter buds the same way. Or press colorful foliage for winter decoration. (See also How to Dry Flowers, How to Press.) As soon as buds swell in early spring, branches may be brought indoors and forced into flower. (See Forcing Flowering Branches.)

Doronicum excelsum (See Leopards-Bane)

DRACAENA (*Dracaena Godseffiana*)

Foliage lasts 2 weeks or longer. Cut where leaves join the plant, taking as much stem as possible. Wash leaves in cold water. Split stem. Condition overnight in cold water.

DUMB-CANE (*Dieffenbachia Seguine*)

Foliage lasts 2 weeks or longer. This will thrive and root in water in a light place. Remove foliage where stem joins plant, taking as long a stem as you can. Condition overnight in cold water. If necessary, to prevent drying and curling, spray foliage with clear plastic on underside *only*.

DUSTY MILLER (*Artemesia Stelleriana*)

The foliage is more useful than the flowers. Split stems. Condition overnight with the initial placement in hot water, 100° F., to start with. Sometimes it takes longer than overnight for foliage to become crisp and turgid. If it does not at first respond to hot water, recut and split again, placing stems in hot water a second time. Two changes should do it, with no more than 24 hours of conditioning for foliage to reach perfect condition.

Dutchmans-Breeches (See Bleeding Heart)
Echinops (See Globe Thistle)

EDGING LOBELIA (*Lobelia Erinus*)

Lasts 4 to 8 days; with roots attached, for 10 days. Lift entire plant when half in flower. Wash soil from roots. Condition overnight with roots in cold water.

Trim away excess foliage and buds. Arrange casually, preferably in low, opaque bowls. Since this lasts so well, it may be combined with similarly treated material: Sweet Alyssum, English Daisies, and Pansies.

EMPRESS TREE (*Paulownia tomentosa*)

Lasts 3 to 5 days. Lavender flowers; brown, coarse-textured seed pods; velvety buds are also possibilities from this tree. Cut panicles when 3 or 4 flowers are open. Some buds will then open in water, although they are not entirely dependable. Split woody stems. Condition overnight with stems in warm water to start with. Collect seed pods in various shades and stages of development. They need not be conditioned.

ENGLISH DAISY (*Bellis perennis*)

Lasts 7 to 10 days. Superior for cutting, the only disadvantage being short stems. Cut flowers when three-quarters to fully open. Split stems for about an inch. Condition overnight in cold water. Revive prematurely wilted flowers by recutting and placing stems in warm water, 80° to 100° F. If you can spare them, lift whole plants with roots attached. Wash away excess soil. Plants last a long while this way, buds continuing to open. If grown in semishade, plants produce slightly longer stems, larger flower-heads, and have a longer blooming period.

Eschscholzia californica (See Poppy, California)

EUCALYPTUS (*Eucalyptus* in variety)

Practically indestructible. The variety obtainable through Eastern florists has gray-green foliage, a unique leaf, and pleasing texture. The leaves clasp and surround stems. Split stems. Condition overnight, or until used, with stems in cold water. Use with fresh or dried material. Treated with glycerin and water, foliage turns a luscious, chocolate brown. (See How to Dry Flowers.)

Eucharis grandiflora (See Amazon-Lily)
Eupatorium coelestinum (See Floss-Flower)
Euphorbia (See Spurge, Flowering)
Euphorbia epithymoides or *E. polychroma* (See Cushion Spurge)
Euphorbia fulgens (See Scarlet Plume)
Euphorbia heterophylla (See Mexican Fire-Plant)
Euphorbia marginata (See Snow-on-the-Mountain)
Euphorbia pulcherrima (See Poinsettia)

EVERGREENS IN VARIETY

This is the Japanese way of treating evergreens and the Japanese excel in caring for plant material: To remove dust or grime, collected perhaps over a period of years, wash foliage and branches in warm soapy water. Rinse in cold water. The breathing or guard cells on underside of leaves will now function efficiently and so give longer life. You may be surprised to see how glossy, alive, and healthy looking evergreens so treated can be. Shellacking, polishing with oil, or rubbing with wax paper now becomes unnecessary. Split woody stems 2 to 3 inches. Place stems in warm water to condition overnight, or longer. Add 1 tablespoon of glycerin to each quart of water for conditioning all-evergreen arrangements. If fresh flowers are used with evergreens, use glycerin *only* for the conditioning of the evergreens.

In winter, after the washing, submerge evergreens in

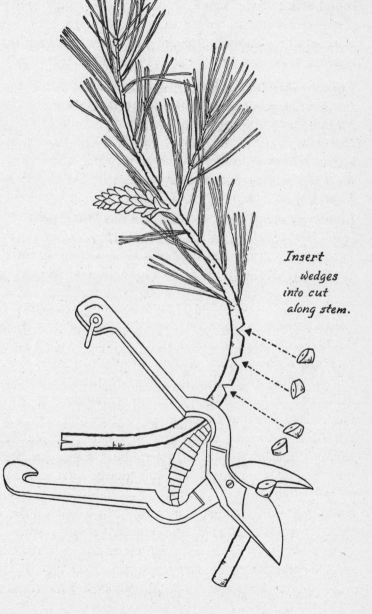

Plate 4

Insert
wedges
into cut
along stem.

cold water for 1 day. This makes them fresh and crisp and banishes the lifeless look common at this season. Immersion also makes stems more pliable, and, if you tie them in desired curves and allow them to dry so before arranging with only their stems in water, the curves will remain. There will be just a little spring-back, so curve stems a little more than desired for the final arrangement.

A further word on how to attain attractive line in heavy materials: Make a thick branch pliable by placing the section to be curved under hot running water. Slowly bend and twist as heat and moisture soften it. (Water should be no hotter than your hand can bear.) It takes about 5 minutes or so. When a branch is stubborn, push aside needles or leaves from the section you are working on, and wrap a hot vinegar-dipped cloth around it to soften the fiber. Bend first from the place on the stem where the center of the curve will come. Keep your thumbs close together on the branch as you bend it, and on the *inside* of the curve. When you get the curve you want, tie it firmly in place and submerge the whole branch in cold water. The curve will then become fixed.

If the branch is unusually thick and woody, you can also make a series of small cuts across the outside of the curve. This makes the branch easier to bend. If cuts seem to go too deep or open further than you wish when the branch is bent, insert sections of stem-wood into the cuts to secure and hold branch in curving position. (See Plate 4.)

It is often wise to fireproof Christmas greens. For 5 minutes, submerge branches in a solution of 1 pound ammonium phosphate (garden-supply house) to 2 gallons of water. This will not turn foliage brown. Do not confuse with ammonium sulphate, unsatisfactory for fireproofing and likely to turn greens brown. (See also Christmas Trees.)

Everlastings (See Dried Flowers)
Fagus (See Beech)
Fairy Primula (See Primrose)

FALSE HOLLY
(*Osmanthus aquifolium* or *Olea ilicifolia*)

Flowers open over a period of 5 to 10 days, foliage lasts 1 to 3 weeks. Insignificant, delightfully fragrant, white flowers are numerous, crowded close to main stem. Cut in the advanced-bud stage and allow to open indoors. Split woody stems. Condition overnight with stems in warm water to start with. After blossoms have faded, foliage can be reused.

FALSE INDIGO (*Baptisia australis*)

Lasts 5 to 7 days. Cut when about one-third of the florets on the lower stem are open. Recut just below a node prior to conditioning overnight with stems in deep cold water. As with Lupine, spray with a fine mist of cold water to retard dropping of buds. In summer and autumn, use the medium-sized inflated seed pods at the green or gun-metal stage. Foliage treated with glycerin and water turns a fine dark-blue.

Feathered Columbine (See Meadow-Rue)
Fennel-Flower (See Love-in-a-Mist)

FERN, ASPARAGUS (*Asparagus* in variety)

There are two types. *Plumosus* with fine dark-green, feathery foliage, once used almost exclusively by florists for foliage, can be refrigerated when cut, with stems out of water. Tied in small bunches and stored at 48° to 50° F., it can be held for 1 to 2 weeks. Upon removal, arrange without first conditioning in water. Unless quite freshly cut, it drops its gauzy green soon after exposure to warm rooms. If you are using large quantities for decoration, and without water, spray sparingly with clear plastic to check dropping. Allow to dry well before using. The coarser, needle-type *Sprengeri* lasts well when cut, up to 2 weeks. Place stems in cold water. Condition overnight, or until used.

FERN, CINNAMON (*Osmunda cinnamomea*)

Lasts 2 to 3 days. Cut when fronds are fully developed. Place in flat container of cold water so they will be completely covered. Remove when crisp, in about 1 hour. Shake off excess water and spread out on newspapers for a few minutes to dry. Then stand upright with stems in cold water, pH 4, until used. This fern may be pressed for use in dried bouquets. (See How to Press Flowers.)

FERN, MAIDENHAIR (*Adiantum cuneatum*)

In tests, it was found that this fern keeps twice as long when *cut* from plants as when *pulled*. Condition by submerging fronds in cold water for 1 to 2 hours. Thereafter, keep stems in cold water until used. Or press Maidenhair for winter bouquets. It can also be skeletonized. (For an interesting way to press, see *'Til Summer Comes Again* by Eleanor Bolton, Fairfax, Virginia.)

FERNS IN VARIETY

Condition fragile types like New York and Interrupted Fern by submerging in cold water in a container to accommodate them *lengthwise* without crowding. Be sure they are completely covered with water. Let remain 2 to 4 hours; longer for the less delicate types like Sensitive and Polypody Fern. Remove, shake free of excess water, and place with stems in cold water until used. For winter bouquets, press ferns as soon as fronds are mature. (See How to Press Flowers.)

FEVERFEW (*Chrysanthemum Parthenium*)

Lasts up to 1 week. Dwarf varieties are fine for small arrangements. Cut when about half the florets are open. Split stems. Condition overnight in warm water to start with.

Fire-Bush (See Quince, Flowering)

FIRETHORN (*Pyracantha coccinea*)

Attractive in two stages, the white blossoms in spring last up to 1 week; the red-orange or yellow fruits in fall should be arranged in water. They keep well if room is not too warm. For easier handling remove thorns at base of stems before conditioning. Remove some leaves so as to show off blooms or fruits to advantage. Split woody stems. Condition overnight with stems in warm water to begin with. Fruits shrivel and drop off when dried. You can prevent this to a degree by spraying with clear plastic.

FLAX (*Linum* in variety)

Lasts 4 to 7 days. Select stems for cutting with a few flowers open on each. Split woody stems. Condition overnight with stems in warm water to start with. Let remain until sufficiently open. I find 24 hours about right for conditioning. Flax then lasts well. Note that it blooms profusely every *other* day. Gather large quantities of budded stalks which will be open 1 to 2 days later.

Floras-Paintbrush (See Tassel-Flower)

FLOSS-FLOWER (*Ageratum Houstonianum*)

Lasts 5 to 7 days. Cut when about half the flowers are open in each cluster. Remaining buds should be showing good color. If cut too early, buds refuse to open. If cut too late, that is, after all the flowers are open, they last such a short time they are not worth the trouble. Condition overnight with stems in warm water to start with. (Often recommended for drying, but I have not found it satisfactory.)

FLOWERING TOBACCO (*Nicotiana affinis*)

Florets last 2 to 3 days, clusters continue opening up to 7 days. The first blooms of the season are best. Cut when 1 or 2 flowers in the loose clusters are fully open; well-developed buds will open in water. Condition overnight with stems in warm water to start with. Growing in semishade extends blooming period and produces slightly larger flowers and more vivid color. (Sun bleaches petals.)

FORGET-ME-NOT (*Myosotis alpestris*)

Lasts up to 5 days. Cut when about half in flower. Condition stems in hot water, 80° to 100° F., to start with. If this does not bring flowers to good condition, recut and dip stem-ends in boiling water for 1½ to 3 minutes, but protect upper leaves and flowers from steam. Follow this by conditioning overnight with stems in cold water. Or, for low arrangements, lift small plants which are about one-fourth in flower. Wash soil from roots. Condition overnight with roots in cold water. Plants will go on blooming for about 1 week.

FORSYTHIA OR GOLDEN BELLS
(*Forsythia* in variety)

Buds keep opening 1 to 3 weeks. Cut branches that are just beginning to flower. Always cut just below or through a node. Stems are hollow in between. (See Plate 1.) Place in cold water. Condition overnight or until sufficiently open. (See also Forcing Flowering Branches.)

FOUR-O'CLOCKS OR MARVEL-OF-PERU
(*Mirabilis Jalapa*)

Not very satisfactory for cutting. Flowers stay closed till late afternoon, but the varicolored buds have interesting uses. Foliage is also good with other flowers. Condition it with stems in cold water overnight.

FOXGLOVE (*Digitalis purpurea*)

Lasts 5 to 10 days. Cut when one-fourth to one-half the flowering spike is open. Very tall stems should be at least half open. Condition overnight with stems in warm water to start with. For curving stems, place slant-wise in container for conditioning period. Remove lower flowers as they fade; shorten stems to balance arrangement. If flower stalks wilt while in the arrangement, remove them, recut, and place stems in hot water until they revive.

Fragrant Plantain (See Plantain Lily)

FRANGIPANI (*Plumeria* in variety)

Florets last 1 to 2 days, buds go on opening for several more. Flowers appear mostly before foliage. Stems contain milky juice. Cut when flowers are half open. Sear stem-ends in a flame for 15 seconds. Then condition overnight with stems in cold water. Petals fall quickly. Dipping flowers in cold water just before arranging gives added freshness.

FRANKLINIA (*Franklinia or Gordonia alatamaha*)

Lasts 2 or 3, sometimes 4 days if taken in bud and allowed to open indoors. Cut when newly open or when large buds are just ready to unfold. They open quickly when sprayed with a fine mist of cold water. Remove foliage not necessary for decoration. Split woody stems. Condition overnight with stems in cold water. Be sure to get flowers before they have been visited by insects; Japanese beetles love them. Tie cellophane bags around well-developed buds to discourage beetles and insure unblemished flowers. Check bags daily for excess moisture which may collect inside and pull bags down against expanding petals.

FREESIA (*Freesia refracta, F. hybrida*)

Florets last 2 to 3 days and clusters continue opening up to the last bud. Cut when first 2 or 3 flowers in each cluster are well opened. Condition overnight with stems in cold water reaching almost to flower-heads. Leave ample room for buds to unfold. Wrap flowers loosely (not individually) in cellophane or thin wax paper to preserve the delicious fragrance until you are ready to arrange. Humidity inside wrapping is beneficial and aids opening of buds. If possible, store at 45° to 50° F. until used. Remove wilted flowers as buds continue to open.

Fritillaria (See Crown Imperial)

FRUIT IN VARIETY

When selecting fruits (vegetables too) for arrangements, look for the firmest and heaviest ones. These are freshest and contain the most moisture. The older fruit is, the lighter it becomes, due to evaporation and drying out of natural juices. If no mechanical aids are used, fruit remains unspoiled and can later be eaten. Wooden picks, skewers, Twistems, and wire are helpful but ultimately damaging. When fresh flowers and foliages are combined with fruit, you can place stems in water-filled orchid tubes and then conceal these in the arrangement. Fruits are more brilliant if thoroughly washed in cold water or cleansed with a damp cloth.

Rosy cheeks can be given green fruits by a strategic rubbing with lipstick. A festive and Christmasy look results if fruits are coated with unbeaten egg white and, while wet, sprinkled generously with fine granulated sugar. Let dry well before using. For long-standing arrangements and Della Robbia wreaths, coat fruit with clear plastic or shellac.

FUCHSIA (*Fuchsia hybrida*)

Flowers last 5 to 7 days, foliage much longer, even to the point of rooting. Select branches with more fully-opened flowers than buds and include a portion of woody stem. Buds do not open well after cutting. Split woody stems. Remove all foliage not necessary for decoration. Hold stem-ends in boiling water for 1½ to 3 minutes. Then place in cold water to condition overnight. I have also had good luck without using boiling water. I add a commercial preservative to conditioning water and then to the water for the arrangement. I always spray flowers and foliage with a fine mist of cold water as soon as branches are cut. This checks moisture-loss. Fuchsia foliage is ideal for mixed bouquets, the reddish and purplish stems and undersides of leaves adding a delicate note.

Fullerweed (See Teazle)
Funkia (See Plantain Lily)
Gaillardia grandiflora (See Blanket-Flower)

GALAX (*Galax aphylla*)

Flowers last 3 to 5 days but are not showy, foliage almost forever. Cut flowers when about one-quarter of the spike is open. Condition overnight with stems in cold water. The durable, leathery leaves, glossy and of subdued color, blend well with other flowers, fruits, and vegetables. Foliage lasts marvelously. Submerge in cold water for about 30 minutes; thereafter keep stems in cold water until used. Submerged in a solution of half-and-half glycerin and water, leaves turn lovely shades of brown and greenish-bronze, remain usable for several seasons.

GARDEN HELIOTROPE (*Valeriana officinalis*)

Lasts 6 to 10 days, depending on stage of development. Cut when only a few florets are open in each cluster. Condition overnight with stems in warm water to start with. When allowed to open indoors, petals do not drop as quickly as outside. Recut stems as necessary.

GARDENIA OR CAPE-JASMINE
(*Gardenia florida* or *G. Fortuniana*)

Lasts 4 to 6 days, depending on heat and humidity. Cut blossoms when fully open. Half-open or even fairly-tight buds open in water and last many days, but then blooms are small and lack color, substance, and texture. If you are cutting from a bush in your garden, split woody stems. Condition overnight in cold water. Spray both flowers and foliage with a fine mist of cold water or submerge in water till petals are crisp. Place florist's short-stemmed flowers on wet cotton; store in a covered box in refrigerator or cool room at a temperature of 45° to 50° F. Petals turn brown when handled carelessly or even touched. It helps to dip flowers and hands in cold water before working with them. (Kenneth Glasgow, a florist, tells me that when he uses Gardenias in low arrangements, he turns the flowers face-down into the water each night and this prolongs their life.)

GAS-PLANT OR BURNING-BUSH
(*Dictamnus fraxinella*)

Lasts 5 to 7 days as florets go on opening. Cut flowering spike when about one-third open; buds will continue to open in water. Split stems. Condition overnight with stems in cold water. Don't overlook the seed pods which are distinctive in form and color. Use them green or dried.

GERANIUM (*Pelargonium* in variety)

Flowers last 5 to 8 days, depending on variety; foliage often stays fresh longer, the stalks even taking root in water. Cut clusters when half in flower. Remove some foliage. Split stems. Condition with stems in cold water overnight. Types with very hairy stems and foliage, like Peppermint and Rose Geranium, wilt more readily. Condition these by first placing in warm water, 80° to 100° F. Dry the sweet-leaved kinds. (See Potpourri.)

GERBERA, TRANSVAAL OR
BARBERTON DAISY (*Gerbera Jamesoni*)

Lasts 5 to 7 days. Cut when fully open, or nearly so, with centers tight and pollen not yet ripe. Buds add interest to arrangements, but flowers are small and less colorful when they open in water. Condition overnight with stems in cold water reaching almost to flowerheads. Gentle curves result when stems are placed slantwise in the container during conditioning. Recondition florist's Gerbera before arranging.

GERMAN CATCHFLY (*Lychnis Viscaria*)

Lasts 4 to 5 days but not very satisfactory for cutting because such a quantity is needed to gain an effect. Cut when one-quarter to one-half the flowering-stem is open. Condition overnight with stems in warm water to begin with.

GEUM (*Geum chiloense* or *G. coccineum*)

Lasts 5 to 7 days. Cut when flowers are about three-fourths open. Condition with stems in warm water to begin with, and let remain overnight. Tight buds will not open in water.

Gilliflower (See Stock)

GLADIOLUS (*Gladiolus* in variety)

Florets last 1 to 2 days; stalks go on blooming 1 to 2 weeks. Cut when second floret is ready to open. Contrary to usual procedure, cut about 2 P.M. when flowers are *slightly* wilted. If you must cut in early morning or evening when flowers are turgid, let them remain out of water a half hour or so until tissues soften. This delays opening of buds. Recut and split stems just before you place them in cold water to remain overnight. Condition at average room temperature. If, while in the bud stage, Gladiolus are kept or stored cool immediately after being cut and then brought to a warm room, life is brief.

Allow ample space for each bud to expand petals. This may seem like overstressing a detail, but if stems and buds are pressed together, petals may be damaged and blossoms will not be shapely. It is surprising how much stems and buds expand in water. The tiny buds at the tips seldom open and may as well be removed at the start unless needed for height.

To avoid having all stiff, straight stems, place some slant-wise in the container while conditioning. Then tips will curve upward. For low arrangements and easy placements, cut some stems into short lengths of 1, 2, or 3 florets. If you must touch petals, wet hands and flowers so as not to bruise them. To get more color, remove outer green covering from several of the buds immediately above the highest open flower. This carries color farther up and avoids the appearance of too many buds and too much green.

GLOBE AMARANTH (*Gomphrena globosa*)

Lasts up to 1 week. Then foliage may be stripped off and blossoms dried. Grown primarily as an everlasting, it is also excellent as a fresh flower. Cut when three-quarters to fully open with yellow stamens showing. Remove foliage not needed for decoration. Split stems. Condition overnight with stems in warm water to start with. Early in the season when growth is soft, flowers respond to this conditioning. Later, stems become woody and flowers do not last so well after cutting. For drying, gather completely open flowers as soon as they have attained their globelike shape. Strip off foliage. Hang to dry. Dye white flowers either while they are still fresh or after they have dried. (See Dyeing Flowers.)

GLOBE-FLOWER (*Trollius europaeus*)

Lasts up to 1 week. For interesting effects, cut at various stages of development, from tight buds to flowers three-quarters open. Well-developed buds will open into full flower after cutting. Split stems 1 to 2 inches. Condition overnight with stems in cold water.

GLOBE THISTLE (*Echinops* in variety)

Lasts up to 1 week. Valuable for its pale-blue coloring. Cut when about one-quarter of the globe is covered with open flowers. Buds open well in water. Split stems. Condition with stems in cold water overnight, or until flowers are sufficiently open. Foliage is coarse, but attractive.

Gloriosa Rothschildiana (See Glory Lily)

GLORY LILY (*Gloriosa Rothschildiana*)

Lasts 4 to 5 days. Gather when flowers are fully open or when petals are partly turned back. Split stems. Condition overnight with stems in cold water. Re-cut stems if base appears coated or slightly soft.

Godetia in variety (See Satinflower)
Gold-Dust Tree (See Aucuba)
Golden Bells (See Forsythia)

GOLDEN-CHAIN TREE
(*Laburnum anagyroides* or *L. vulgare*)

Lasts 1 to 3 days. Gather clusters when one-half open, pruning carefully as you cut. Remove foliage not necessary for decoration. Split woody stems. Condition overnight with stems in warm water to start with.

GOLDEN MARGUERITE (*Anthemis tinctoria*)

Lasts 7 to 10 days. Cut stems with a few fully-opened flowers. Condition overnight with stems in cold water. Cut foliage anytime after it has attained sufficient length and place some stems slantwise in a low, wide-mouthed container during conditioning period. They will assume beautiful curves.

GOLDEN-RAIN TREE (*Koelreuteria paniculata*)

Lasts 3 to 4 days. Cut when flower clusters are about half open. Split woody stems. Remove foliage not necessary for decoration. Condition overnight with stems in warm water to start with. Also gather seed pods as soon as they are formed. If cut at an early stage, light-green fruits should be placed with stems in cold water for several hours. If cut later in the season, when practically dried, they need not be conditioned.

GOLDENROD (*Solidago canadensis*)

Lasts 1 to 3 weeks and then may be dried. Satisfactory at any stage. Develops well in water if cut when but a few florets are open. Condition with stems in cold water for at least 4 hours, but preferably overnight. For drying, cut when fully open. Goldenrod retains color and shape almost perfectly, turning a rich, mellow, truly-golden shade. Properly dried, it can be used for several years. *Solidago bicolor*, Silverod, has white flowers.

Golden-Tuft (See Basket-of-Gold)
Gomphrena globosa (See Globe Amaranth)
Gordonia alatamaha (See Franklinia)

GOURDS IN VARIETY

Gather when outer shells are hard and with a portion of stem attached. This will be at the end of the growing season after foliage has withered. To remove any clinging soil, wash in a solution of Sylpho Napthol. (Available at drugstores in liquid form. Use 1 teaspoon to each quart of water.) If possible, dry in the sun for a few days. Then store in a dry, cold (not freezing) place where there is free circulation of air. To insure against decay within, make one small hole through outer shell into center. Pierce with a fine electric drill or very thin nail. When gourds are well dried, coat with clear plastic or shellac, if you wish. This makes them last almost indefinitely. Or cover with a dull, flat paint or a glossy, highlighted enamel. Large gourds make interesting hanging containers when dried, hollowed out, and waterproofed. These are seen in many old oriental prints. The gourds are embellished with thin leather straps or decorative cord.

GRAPE IVY (*Cissus rhombifolia*)

Lasts for weeks. Condition by submerging mature foliage in cold water for at least 2 hours, or it may remain overnight. (Young, tender foliage should not be submerged more than 1 hour.) Remove and place stems in cold water until used. Keep this foliage fresh in vegetable or fruit arrangements by inserting stems in water-filled orchid tubes.

GUERNSEY LILY (*Nerine sariensis* hybrids)

Florets last 1 to 3 days; cluster goes on opening while there are buds. Cut flowers when clusters are half open. Split stems. Condition overnight with stems in cold water. Autumnal blooms appear on leafless stems reaching up to 30 inches.

Gypsophila (See Babys-Breath)
Hardhack (See Spirea)
Heartsease (See Pansy)

HEATHER (*Calluna* in variety)

True Scotch Heather, *Calluna vulgaris*, lasts almost indefinitely, retaining its color, with stems in or out of water. Most arrangers prefer to use it with stems in water. For this purpose, remove the small leaves and flowers extending below the water-level. If flowering tips collapse, split stems and place in warm water, 80° to 100° F. For dried arrangements, hang heather upside-down in the usual manner.

Hedera helix (See Ivy, English)
Helianthus decapetalus (See Sunflower)

HELIOTROPE (*Heliotropium peruvianum*)

Lasts 3 to 5 days. Cut when half to three-quarters of the cluster is open. If possible, include a portion of woody stem. Split stems and condition overnight with stem-ends in hot water, 100° F., to start with. If flowers do not look fresh and turgid by the time water has cooled, place stem-ends again in hot water. Foliage is discolored and damaged by hot water so keep it well above water-level. Cut and condition stems of various lengths to avoid recutting when arranging. If necessary to recut, the hot-water treatment must be applied to the new cuts,

or they must be seared in a flame for 15 seconds. (See also
Garden Heliotrope, *Valeriana officinalis*.)

Helleborus niger (See Christmas Rose)
Hemerocallis (See Daylily)
Hepatica (See Liverleaf)
Herb of Grace (See Rue)

HERBS IN VARIETY

Herbs, decorative with cut flowers or alone,
keep better than most cut foliages. Select foliage that does
not appear tender; avoid new growth. Strip foliage from
base of stems and split them. Most herbs have woody
stems, especially toward the end of the growing season.
Place stems in warm water. Allow to remain overnight.
Spray foliage with a fine mist of cool water to prevent too
much loss of moisture through the many leaves. (See also
separate listings of Bee-Balm, Lavender, Rosemary.)

THESE HERBS ARE FINE FOR CUTTING:

Angelica (*Angelica Archangelica*)
Basil, Sanctum and Sweet (*Ocimum*)
Bergamot (See Bee-Balm)
Bugle-Weed (*Ajuga reptans*)
Caraway (*Carum Carvi*)
Catnip or Catmint (*Nepeta sp.*)
Chives (*Allium Schoenoprasum*)
Dill (*Anethum graveolens*)
Fennel (*Foeniculum*)
Germander (*Teucrium Chamaedrys*)
Hyssop (*Hyssopus officinalis*)
Lavender Cotton
   (*Santolina Chamaecyparissus*)
Lemon Balm (*Melissa officinalis*)

Lovage (*Levisticum officinale*)
Marjoram (*Marjorana sp.* or *Origanum sp.*)
Mint (*Mentha sp.*)
Mugwort (*Artemesia sp.*)
Mullein (*Verbascum sp.*)
Parsley (*Petroselinum sp.*)
Pennyroyal (*Mentha Pulegium*)
Tarragon, French
    (*Artemesia Dracunculus*)
Thyme (*Thymus sp.*)

Hesperis matronalis (See Sweet Rocket)
Heuchera sanguinea (See Coral-Bells)

HIBISCUS (*Hibiscus* in variety)

Lasts 1 to 2 days. When cut, these exotic flowers last as long out of water as they do in. Since their life span is brief, gather just before arranging. If you have plants of some size, cut long stems, split them, and condition in cold water for at least 4 hours. For drying, use Borax and sand. (See How to Dry Flowers.)

Hibiscus Moscheutos or *H. palustris* (See Rose-Mallow)
Hibiscus syriacus (See Althea)
Hippeastrum Reginae (See Amaryllis)

HOLLY (*Ilex* in variety)

Lasts for weeks. Cut preferably when fruits are fully developed and color is brilliant, whether green, red, or yellow. You *can* cut at any time of year though hardly when trees are dropping leaves or before new foliage has fully developed. Split woody stems. Condition overnight, or up to 24 hours or longer. In winter, submerge branches of evergreen holly in cold water for 8 hours to overnight to rid foliage of dust or grime. After conditioning, holly can be sprayed with clear plastic or shellac. This checks evaporation, delays curling and dropping, but it does give a polished, artificial look.

To save berries when birds feed heavily on your trees and shrubs, cut branches with ripe fruits and keep in a cool, dark place with stems plunged in cold water. Use large containers of wood, agate, earthenware, or porcelain but not metal.

HOLLYHOCK (*Althea rosea*)

Florets may last 2 to 3 days and open on a full stalk over a period of 5 to 9 days; that is, sometimes they do; again they droop for no apparent reason. The pH of soil and water is evidently an important factor. Hollyhocks are most dependable if cut late in the afternoon or early in the morning with 3 or 4, or even half, the blooms open on the stem. Well-developed buds will open in water; tight buds will not. Remove all but the smallest leaves near the tip of the flowering stalk; if these leaves are of considerable size, take them off also. Split stems for 5 or 6 inches. Sear ends in a flame while you count to 15 slowly. Then condition overnight, or for a day or two longer, until more blossoms are open, with stems in a generous amount of warm water to start with. Double hollyhocks will last longer than singles as it takes longer for all the petals to unfold. Both are ideal for large, fan-shaped arrangements in front of a fireplace in summer and also for low bowls. For these, long stems are cut into sections of 1, 2, or 3 flowers each.

Experiments published in a *Journal* of the Royal Horticultural Society indicate that Hollyhocks are benefited by being kept in a weak solution of potassium nitrate—1 part to 1,000, or a pinch to each quart of water (obtainable at drugstore).

HONESTY, MOONWORT, PENNY- OR SATIN-FLOWER (*Lunaria annua* or *L. biennis*)

Flowers last 5 to 7 days. Primarily grown for the silvery fruits which are dried for winter bouquets. For fresh arrangements, cut long stems when clusters are half open. Condition overnight with stems in warm water to begin with. For drying, let flowers remain on plants until seed pods mature. Cut when these are past the soft-green stage and beginning to turn tan and dry. Tie in small bunches and hang. When sufficiently dried—it may take 4 weeks or more—carefully remove the tannish-green paper covering from each side of the parchment-like silvery disc. To do this, hold a pod between thumb and forefinger, pinch slightly, and slide off both sides of the covering at the same time. The seeds are lodged between the disc and the outer covering which you remove.

HONEYSUCKLE (*Lonicera* in variety)

Flowers last 4 to 7 days, depending on variety. Cut branches with a portion of old wood and when about half the flower clusters are open along about a quarter of the branch. (Some Honeysuckles grow more like shrubs than vines and send forth fairly long stems with 1 or 2 flower clusters at the tip. Cut these when less than half the flowers are open.) Split woody stems and condition overnight in cold water.

Hordeum vulgare (See Barley)
Hosta (See Plantain Lily)

HOUSELEEKS OR SUCCULENTS
   (*Sempervivum* in variety)

Flowers last 7 to 10 days, foliage up to 3 weeks. Crassulas, some Echeverias, and Hen-and-Chickens will keep without benefit of water. When you need long sections of stem, cut and submerge pieces for about half an hour beforehand. When used with no fresh material, arrange Houseleeks without water to prevent decay of stems.

Houstonia caerulea (See Bluets)

HYACINTH, DUTCH OR ROMAN
   (*Hyacinthus orientalis*)

Lasts 3 to 6 days. When fully open or nearly so, cut Hyacinths preferably above the white portion at the base of the stems. Use a very sharp knife. Split stems—unless they split of their own accord—and place in cold water overnight. If longer stems are needed, include the white area, but split up into the green part before conditioning. A Twistem tied around a stem holds parts together and facilitates arranging. If Hyacinths wilt prematurely, dip stem-ends in boiling water for 1½ to 3 minutes. Then put stems in cold water and condition overnight. You can capture the lovely fragrance by wrapping the bouquet of flower-heads (not the individual clusters) in thin wax paper during conditioning. (See also Summer Hyacinth, *Galtonia candicans*.)

HYACINTH, GRAPE (*Muscari* in variety)

Lasts 3 to 6 days. Take when a quarter to a half open. For long stems, pull, don't cut, stalks from plants but be careful not to uproot. Split stems, unless they split naturally, and place in cold water overnight. Stems will then elongate somewhat and buds open. For interesting curves, place stems in ice water at the start.

HYDRANGEA (*Hydrangea* in variety)

Lasts 4 to 9 days depending on type. Cut when half the panicle is open. Split stems about 1 inch. Remove foliage not necessary for decoration. Hold stem-ends in 2 or 3 inches of boiling vinegar, and count slowly to 30 before removing; or sear stem-ends in a flame for 15 seconds. Either way, condition overnight with stems in deep cold water adjusted to pH 4. (Vinegar helps lower pH, and the heat expands the wood vessels.) Water on the petals helps. Submerge the big flower-heads in cold water until crisp. If they are almost completely open when cut, they are difficult to keep. Many types dry well, especially *H. paniculata grandiflora* and *H. quercifolia*. Cut for drying when the sterile flowers turn crisp and papery.

Hypericum (See Saint Johns-Wort)
Iberis (See Candytuft)
Ilex (See Holly)
Impatiens Balsamina (See Balsam)
Indian Turnip (See Jack-in-the-Pulpit)
Ipomaea purpurea (See Morning-Glory)

IRIS (*Iris* in variety)

For German, Japanese, Siberian types: Flowers last 1 to 2 days, as buds continue to open. Cut when the first bud is ready to unfold. It will be fully open by morning if cut at this stage in late afternoon. Indoors, buds lower on the stem open into somewhat smaller and paler, but still beautiful, blossoms. Fully-opened blooms are so easily damaged by wind, rain, and insects that cutting at the bud stage is all the more advantageous.

For Dutch, English, and Spanish Iris: Blossoms last 3 to 5 days as buds continue to open. These are noted for their keeping qualities. Cut after the first flower unfolds. Other buds on the same stem will open in water. These have more substance than those of Bearded Iris. No Iris blossom can stand a sudden change of temperature, and nothing is gained by placing buds or flowers in cold storage. Tests indicated that when Iris were kept in dry cold storage for 1 week at 32° or 40° F. the lasting quality was reduced to 1 day after removal from storage to a room of 70° F. (Buds and open flowers of Wedgewood Iris were used for this test.)

IVY, ENGLISH (*Hedera helix*)

Lasts for months, even takes root in water. This versatile foliage, with literally hundreds of variations in habit of growth, leaf-contour, veining, and shading of green blends with practically all flowers, fruits, and vegetables. Cut stems just below a node or swelling. Let no leaves remain below the water-line in the container if you expect the spray to take root. It must have a clean growing medium. Thoroughly wash foliage. Condition by submerging in cold water 2 to 4 hours. If stems are of recent growth and appear pale-green and tender at tips, submerge in cold water for 2 to 4 hours so they won't wilt. Do not submerge longer or foliage may deteriorate. Then place stems in cold water until used. You can get Ivy to assume nice lines by tieing sprays in desired curves before submerging. Let dry while still tied.

In more or less permanent arrangements of Ivy, as for churches or public rooms, keep water sweet by placing in the container a few pieces of charcoal (washed to remove soot). Change water as frequently as it gets cloudy.

If you have difficulty rooting Ivy in water, it may be due to purifying agents in the water-supply. If you use well-water, it may not have a beneficial pH. Try rain-water with which I have had complete success for rooting.

Ivy, Grape (See Grape Ivy)

IXIA (*Ixia* hybrids)

Florets last 2 to 3 days; buds continue opening. Recut stems of florist's Ixia before reconditioning in cold water for 2 to 3 hours. If you grow your own, cut when first 2 or 3 florets are fully open. Condition overnight with stems in cold water, or until enough blossoms have opened.

JACK-IN-THE-PULPIT OR INDIAN TURNIP (*Arisaema triphyllum*)

Lasts 4 to 7 days. Cut after the hood is developed and lifted free and above the spadix. Condition overnight with stems in cold water where they will elongate considerably. Allow plenty of room for further stretching after arranging. Colorful fruits form a cluster of brilliant red berries atop the straight stem, like red-coated soldiers standing guard in the woodland.

JACOBINIA (*Jacobinia* in variety)

Lasts up to 5 days. Cut these very showy flowers when bud-tips are showing color. Split woody stems and defoliate judiciously. Place stems in warm water and let remain overnight, or until far enough open.

JADE PLANT (*Crassula* in variety)

Flowers continue opening for 7 to 10 days, foliage lasts up to 3 weeks. Cut blossoms when half the cluster is open. Condition with stems in cold water overnight. Sections of the thick, fleshy foliage are decorative in all-green arrangements with cacti or other succulents. Submerge foliage for about half an hour. It can then be used successfully out of water.

Japanese Anemone (See Anemone)

JERUSALEM CHERRY (*Solanum Pseudo-capsicum*)

Cut branches any time after fruits are formed, from the green stage on. Remove foliage not necessary for decoration. Split stems, and condition in cold water overnight.

Jews-Mallow (See Kerrybush)
Jonquil (See Daffodil)

JUPITERS-BEARD (*Centranthus rubra*)

Lasts up to 7 days. Cut flower clusters when about one-quarter to one-half open. Split stems. Condition with stems in cold water overnight or until flowers are open. Beautiful in early-bud stage but cannot always be depended upon to open fully from there on.

Kalmia latifolia (See Laurel)
Kerria japonica (See Kerrybush)

KERRYBUSH (*Kerria japonica*)

Flowers last up to 5 days as buds continue to open. Take branches half in flower and prune as you cut. Remove stems right down to the ground; on this shrub they will die back anyway rather than put forth new upper growth. Split woody stems. Remove foliage along stems in between blossoms if it is not necessary for decoration. Condition overnight with stems in cold water.

Kniphofia Uvaria or *hybrida* (See Torch-Lily)
Koelreuteria paniculata (See Golden-Rain Tree)
Laburnum anagyroides (See Golden-Chain Tree)
Lady-Slipper (See Balsam)
Laganaria japonica (See Quince, Flowering)
Lagerstroemia indica (See Crape-Myrtle)

LANTANA (*Lantana Camara*)

Flowers continue opening up to 6 days. Cut when outer 3 or 4 rows of flowers in each cluster are fully open. Include a portion of woody stem. Split stems, condition in hot water, 80° to 100° F. Buds open completely in water. It may take more than one placement in hot water to make foliage crisp.

LARKSPUR OR ROCKET LARKSPUR
(*Delphinium Ajacis*)

Lasts up to 10 days as buds continue to open. Time depends largely on weather and humidity. Cut when flowering spikes are one-quarter to one-half open. Buds unfold beautifully after cutting. Condition overnight with stems in cold water. Adjust water to pH 4. If season is unusually hot and dry and all flowers seem to be bursting open at the same time, cut stems when the first 2 or 3 lower florets are open. Place stems in cold water in large containers in a light, cool room. Flowers will now outlast those in the garden and can be arranged as they open properly. Add a few pieces of charcoal to the water when flowers are kept for a long time. Watch condition of stems and recut as necessary. Let no foliage remain below water-level; remove all you can spare above it. Take off faded flowers before they shatter. For drying, cut when stalks are about three-quarters open. Individual florets at base of stems should be fully open and in perfect condition. If lower blossoms shrivel and drop, this part of the stem is a total loss when stalk is dried.

Lathyrus (See Sweet Pea)

LAUREL, MOUNTAIN-LAUREL OR
CALICO-BUSH (*Kalmia latifolia*)

Flowers last up to 2 weeks, foliage for 4 weeks. Cut foliage at any time of year. Cut flowers as they begin to open. Split woody stems. Condition overnight with stems in warm water to begin with. Submerge young, pale-green foliage in cold water about 1 hour before conditioning. Add a few pieces of charcoal to evergreen arrangements to help keep water sweet and fresh. (See also Evergreens.)

Lavatera trimestris (See Tree-Mallow)

LAVENDER (*Lavandula Spica or L. officinalis*)

Lasts up to 10 days. For use in fresh arrangements, cut flowers when about one-half the spike is open. Cut foliage separately. Split stems. Condition overnight with stems in warm water to start with. For drying, cut flowers when three-quarters to fully open. Allow to dry completely by spreading on sheets of newspaper. The flowers will fall from stems. Store in glass jars until used. (See How to Dry Flowers, also Potpourri.)

LEMON-VERBENA
(*Lippia citriodora* or *Aloysia citriodora*)

Lasts up to 7 days. Cut flower panicles when they are one-quarter to one-half open. Split woody stems and condition overnight in hot water, 80° to 100° F., to start with. Spray flowers and foliage with a fine mist of cold water when you place them aside for conditioning. This keeps them fresh longer, as does defoliating to some degree. Leaves retain their fragrance when dried for potpourri.

Leopard-Lily (See Blackberry-Lily)

LEOPARDS-BANE (*Doronicum excelsum*)

Lasts up to 12 days. Cut flowers when petals are turned back but centers are still tight. Buds are decorative at various stages; only advanced buds will open fully after cutting. Condition overnight with stems in cold water almost up to flower-heads. Plan for a few curving stems by placing some slantwise in container.

LEUCOTHOE (*Leucothoe catesbaei*)

Flowers last 7 to 10 days, foliage up to 3 weeks. Especially good for long-lasting or "busy-day" arrangements. Cut flowers when about three-quarters of the raceme is open. Cut foliage at any time. Split stems of both flowering and foliage branches. Condition overnight with stems in cold water. Treat foliage in glycerin and water, or press some for winter use. (See How to Dry Flowers, How to Press.)

LILAC (*Syringa* in variety)

Lasts up to 1 week. Can be cut and held in a cool, dark room up to 2 weeks. Cut when one-fourth to one-half the panicle is open. Remove all foliage from flowering branches. Split woody stems at base. Pull away outer bark for 3 to 4 inches from the base of the stem. Place stems in cold water and let remain overnight, or until panicle is sufficiently opened. Encourage buds to open by spraying with a fine mist of cold water. Cut non-flowering branches to arrange with flowering stems. Split stems and condition overnight in cold water. Lilacs from the florist, lovely European imports, are cut in bud, flown across the ocean, and sold in our shops looking fresh and beautiful. When cut in *early* stages, lilacs are one of the finest and most rewarding flowers. Do not hesitate to cut lilacs from established bushes. Panicles that go to seed draw heavily on the strength of shrubs. Cutting flowers insures stronger plants, more beautiful flowers each successive year.

Lilium longiflorum eximium (See Lily, Easter)
Lilium Martagon (See Lily, Turks-Cap)
Lilium speciosum (See Lily, Rubrum)

LILY, CALLA (*Zantedeschia* in variety)

Flowers last up to 1 week; buds and foliage keep a little longer. Cut or buy at various stages of bud and blossom. Condition with stems in cold water for only about 4 hours, unless convenient to let remain longer. Submerge foliage—stems and leaves—in cold water for 1 to 2 hours. Remove, and thereafter keep stems in cold water until used. Recut ends of stems as necessary. You can bend foliage and flower-stems into desired curves with warm hands. If stems split and curl at base after being in water, wrap a Twistem or rubber band around each to hold it together. This makes it easier to insert on pinholder when arranging. Be sure to keep water-supply adequate if you use a shallow container.

LILY, CANNA (*Canna* in variety)

Florets last 2 to 3 days, buds continue opening. Foliage lasts 10 days, sometimes longer. Cut when the first 2 florets are open. Buds develop well after cutting. Submerge flower and stem until all parts are crisp. Then split stems and place in cold water to condition overnight. If a more colorful effect is desired at the start, cut when more florets are open. The reddish-green, green, or bronze foliage is long lasting when cut and adaptable to large-scale arrangements. Split stems of foliage; then submerge in cold water for half an hour; thereafter, keep stems in cold water until used.

LILY, EASTER
(*Lilium longiflorum eximium* or *L. Harrisi*)

Lasts 5 to 8 days. Cut when 2 or 3 flowers in each cluster or on each stem are open. Split stems and condition in cold water overnight. Keep inside of trumpet clean by removing ripe pollen from anthers before it falls. (If this seems to detract from the natural beauty, consider the purpose. Fallen pollen discolors the inside throat of the flower.) It has been suggested that removing pollen prolongs the life of the flower. Tests show no positive results.

Lily-of-the-Nile (See *Agapanthus*)

LILY, RUBRUM (*Lilium speciosum*)

Lasts 5 to 8 days. Cut after petals turn back, and recut stems under water. Split and condition overnight with stems in cold water.

LILY, TURKS-CAP (*Lilium Martagon*)

Clusters last 5 to 8 days as buds continue to unfold. Flowers are so numerous it is difficult to say when to cut. You can start cutting when the first few flowers have opened or wait until almost all the stalk is in bloom. Split stems. Condition overnight with stems in cold water. The brownish pollen stains clothing and skin, so handle with care. Remove any pollen that falls on furniture as soon as possible; it cuts through wax finishes and is difficult to remove if left to dry.

LILY-OF-THE-VALLEY (*Convallaria majalis*)

Lasts 3 to 7 days. Cut when about one-fourth the spray is open and buds are showing color all the way to the tip. Buds open beautifully in water and seem to be more fragrant than when allowed to mature outdoors. Condition overnight with stems in cold water. To preserve fragrance, wrap whole bouquet loosely in thin wax paper or cellophane while flowers are being conditioned.

Flowers used in bridal bouquets and corsages which must keep fresh while out of water are treated thus: After stems have been in water for at least 8 hours, a very fine threadlike wire is wrapped around each stem from base to tip. Then stems are hung upside-down in a florist's or ice refrigerator for 3 to 6 hours prior to using. In this way water gravitates to the very tips of the stems and freshness is assured.

Limonium latifolium (See Sea-Lavender)
Limonium sinuatum (See Statice)
Linum (See Flax)
Lippia citriodora (See Lemon-Verbena)
Little Owl (See Butterfly)
Live-Forever (See *Sedum*)

LIVERLEAF (*Hepatica triloba* or *H. americana*)

Lasts 3 to 5 days. Cultivated and double forms are now available and the small flowers are lovely for cutting. Gather when newly opened. Split stems. Condition both flowers and leaves overnight with stems in warm water to start with. (See also treatment for African Violets.)

Lobelia cardinalis (See Cardinal-Flower)
Lobelia siphilitica (See Blue Lobelia)
Lobularia maritima (See Sweet Alyssum)
Lonicera (See Honeysuckle)
Lotus (See Waterlily)

LOVE-IN-A-MIST OR FENNEL-FLOWER
(*Nigella damascena*)

Lasts 7 to 10 days. Cut stems when central flower and perhaps 1 or 2 more are open; surrounding buds will be at various stages of development. Condition overnight with stems in a 5 per cent solution of sugar. Use 4 teaspoons sugar to each quart of warm water. Inflated seed pods are green, turning tan to brown in late autumn. Cut these in various shades for unusual touches to mixed bouquets. If taken green, they should be conditioned with stems in water overnight. Or you can dry them for winter use. (See How to Dry Flowers.)

LOVE-LIES-BLEEDING (*Amaranthus caudatus*)

Lasts up to 1 week. Cut foliage when leaves have developed size, shape, and color desired; excellent for mixed summer bouquets. Cut flowers at any stage. Condition overnight with stems in cold water. Blossoms dry well, but are difficult to arrange because of their drooping habit.

Lunaria (See Honesty)

LUPINE (*Lupinus polyphyllus*)

Lasts up to 7 days as buds continue to open. Cut when flowering spike is half, or slightly less than half, open. Remove foliage not necessary for decoration and let as much as possible remain on the growing plants. Condition overnight with split stems in cold water. It is common for cut lupines to drop buds or shrivel on the stem before opening. This may be due to method of growing, but the condition can be somewhat corrected by spraying a fine mist of cold water on stems and flowers when you put them aside to condition. Stems curve, but only slightly, when conditioned slantwise in container.

Lupinus polyphyllus (See Lupine)
Lychnis Chalcedonica (See Maltese Cross)
Lychnis Coronaria (See Mullein Pink)
Lychnis Dioica (See Morning Campion)
Lychnis Flos Cuculi (See Ragged Robin)
Lychnis Viscaria (See German Catchfly)
Lycoris radiata (See Amaryllis, Summer)
Lythrum Salicaria (See Purple Loosestrife)
Macleaya cordata (See Plumepoppy)
Madagascar Jasmine (See *Stephanotis*)
Madagascar Periwinkle (See Periwinkle, Madagascar)

MAGNOLIA (*Magnolia* in variety)

Flowers last up to 4 days, sometimes taking 2 days to open fully. Cut well-developed buds. The largest and most advanced will open fully. Small buds become less-perfect flowers. Split woody stems. Scrape bark away from base. Let remain in cold water overnight to condition or until buds unfold. *Soulangeaena* and *Liliflora* varieties last particularly well. If frost threatens when these are ready to burst into flower, cut branches, as trees can spare them, and allow to open indoors. After flowering, the foliage appears.

Magnolia grandiflora, the Southern Magnolia, is strikingly beautiful but, after blossoms open, they usually stay fresh but 1 day, perhaps 2 if weather is humid and cool. Select *well-developed* buds and allow to open indoors. Cut in late afternoon, and they will be fully open by morning. *Tight* buds require several days to open. Submerge open flowers in cold water until petals are crisp and firm. Then lift and place stems in water until arranged. Handle carefully; petals bruise and brown at the slightest touch. It helps to dip flowers and hands in water before you start arranging. You can get the large buds of Southern Magnolia to open when you wish if you unfold petals gently under cold water. This takes practice since petals tear and bruise easily, but often it is a convenience if full-blown flowers are required. These will last several days, but they are not so handsome as blossoms that open naturally. You can also treat foliage in glycerin and water (see How to Dry Flowers). Treat *Magnolia glauca* "the miniature Southern Magnolia," the same way. (To condition foliage of evergreen Magnolias, see Evergreens.)

Maidenhair Fern (See Fern, Maidenhair)

MALTESE CROSS (*Lychnis chalcedonica*)

Flowers last up to 7 days as buds continue to open. Freshness is prolonged by placing stems in a 5 per cent sugar solution—4 teaspoons sugar to each quart of warm water is about right. Cut when slightly less than half the flowers in each cluster are open. Split and condition overnight with stems in the warm solution.

Malus in variety (See Apple Blossom)

MAPLE (*Acer* in variety)

Flowers open over a period of 1 to 2 weeks. Few of us can identify the blossoms of Maple trees, but they are worthy of wider acquaintance. The yellow blooms of Norway Maple and red flowers of Sugar Maple force well in late winter or if cut from trees in early spring when buds are beginning to open. Red Maple has interesting flowers and foliage. All are welcome companions for daffodils and other spring-flowering bulbs. The foliage of Japanese Maple ranges from pale-yellow to deep-red, mahogany, and bronze. Foliage of all of these can be forced into leaf long before the normal season outdoors. Split woody stems. Condition overnight with stems in warm water to start with to which 2 to 4 teaspoons of sugar has been added for each quart. Press the colorful autumn foliage. (See How to Press Flowers.)

MARGUERITE, BOSTON OR PARIS DAISY (*Chrysanthemum frutescens*)

Lasts 6 to 12 days. Select flowers completely open with tight centers. If centers appear powdery, flowers are almost spent. Recut stems under cold water and condition in same water overnight or longer; 24 hours is beneficial. When arranging, allow ample room for lengthening of stems and for flowers to show off their pretty faces.

MARIGOLD (*Tagetes* in variety)

Lasts 1 to 2 weeks, depending on variety. Dwarf and tall kinds make wonderful cut flowers, and keep fresh unusually well. Cut when petals are reflexed, but while centers are tight. This stage is difficult to determine with very double flowers, but these should be about three-quarters open. Buds develop slowly, and not too successfully, after cutting. A small loss of water at the start checks maturation, as with Gladiolus, so it is not imperative to get Marigolds into water immediately. Remember to recut stems under water just before conditioning overnight in cold water. Zinc sulphate (drugstore) is known to retard decay of stems in water. Use 1 teaspoonful of the crystals to each quart of water.

Marvel-of-Peru (See Four-O'Clocks)
Mathiola incana (See Stock)

MAY-APPLE (*Podophyllum peltatum*)

Lasts 3 to 5 days. Flowers usually open by May first, but are hidden under large, umbrella-like leaves. In arranging, remove the large leaf to expose the flowers. Split stems. Condition overnight in cold water. Submerge foliage in cold water ½ to 1 hour; then keep stems in water until used.

MEADOW-RUE OR FEATHERED COLUMBINE (*Thalictrum* in variety)

Flowers last 5 to 10 days. Cut when first buds in cluster are beginning to open. Let remain with stems in cold water until blooms open, or use in the bud stage and enjoy watching flowers unfold in an arrangement. The dark-green or blue-gray foliage lasts up to 2 weeks. Cut foliage at any stage and condition overnight with stems in cold water. (Columbine devotees grow this for its foliage to spare Columbine foliage whose removal weakens plants.)

Mertensia virginica (See Virginia Bluebell)

MEXICAN FIRE-PLANT OR ANNUAL POINSETTIA (*Euphorbia heterophylla*)

Lasts 1 to 2 weeks. Cut when brilliant color is showing on upper leaves, but before the small central blooms have completely opened. (The bright portion at the top is not the flower but a highly-colored area of foliage.) The small flowers are clustered in the center of the top rosette of leaves. Let the flowers be your guide to cutting. Cut when center cluster shows 7 or 8 buds and 1 or 2 completely opened flowers. Stems are hollow and contain a small quantity of milky juice but searing is not necessary. Just split stems and condition overnight in cold water.

MEXICAN SUNFLOWER (*Tithonia* hybrids)

Lasts 5 to 9 days. Invaluable for cutting. Cut just after flowers have fully opened but before pollen has developed in center of blooms. Condition flowers and foliage overnight with stems in warm water to start with. For added interest, cut buds in various stages. Foliage lasts well when cut. Avoid wetting flower petals and foliage. Supply all water through base of stems.

Michaelmas Daisy (See Aster, Hardy)

MIGNONETTE (*Reseda odorata*)

Lasts 5 to 7 days. Cut flowers when about one-quarter or slightly less than one-half the spike is open. Condition overnight with stems in hot water, 80° to 100° F., to start with. Excellent for winter bouquets. For drying, cut when most flowers are fully open, but before those at base of stalk begin to fade. This may be before buds at tip are open. (See How to Dry Flowers.) This is a favorite, too, for bringing fragrance to potpourri. (See Potpourri.)

Milfoil (See Yarrow)

MILKWEED (*Asclepias* in variety)

Lasts 4 to 6 days. Cut when about half open. Sear each stem in a flame for 15 seconds to prevent wilting. Remove foliage not needed for decoration. The birdlike seed pods with their silky interior are fine for dried bouquets. Their development can be arrested at various stages by spraying with clear plastic or coating with shellac, but then a somewhat artificial look results. If you do not wish seed pods to open, gather them early in the season when past the green stage but still tightly closed. If cut early enough, some pods will remain closed even without the spraying.

Mimosa (See Acacia)
Mirabilis Jalapa (See Four-O'Clocks)
Mist-Flower (See Floss-Flower)

MISTLETOE (*Viscum* or *Phoradendron flavescens*)

Mistletoe for market is cut when outdoor temperatures are low. It grows as a parasite on trees. It is kept fresh by refrigeration and without water. If it is not wrapped in cellophane or plastic when you buy it, you wrap it and keep it refrigerated until used. Otherwise split stems and condition overnight in cold water. When it is to be hung or used in decorations without water, dip stem-ends in melted wax, or spray the whole thing with clear plastic to prevent shriveling of foliage and falling of berries. It does not keep well in warm, dry rooms.

MOCKORANGE (*Philadelphus coronarius*)

Lasts 5 to 10 days as buds go on opening. Blooms on second-year wood. Cut when one-quarter of the blossoms along a branch are open. Use sharp shears, pruning and shaping as you cut. Remove at least three-fourths of the foliage. Split stems. Condition overnight, or until sufficiently open, with stems in warm water to start with. Removing foliage makes flowers last longer, displays them more beautifully. If you wish to use the foliage, cut some branches without flowers and condition in the same manner, removing only the non-decorative leaves. If shrubs are well grown, do not hesitate to cut generously early in the season. Shrubs should be pruned soon after blooming anyway to encourage new growth which will bear flowers the following spring.

Molucella laevis (See Bells-of-Ireland)
Monarda didyma (See Bee-Balm)

MONKSHOOD (*Aconitum* in variety)

Lasts 5 to 7 days. Cut when one-third to one-half the spike is in flower. Split stems. Condition overnight with stems in cold water. *Aconitum Napellus* blooms late summer, has dark-blue flowers.

Moonwort (See Honesty)
Moraea iridioides (See Butterfly)

MORNING CAMPION (*Lychnis dioica*)

Lasts 4 to 6 days. Cut hollow stems when there are about as many buds as there are open flowers. Condition overnight with stems in warm water to start with. Remove foliage not necessary for decorations.

MORNING-GLORY (*Convolvulus* or *Ipomaea* in variety)

Lasts 1 to 2 days but buds continue to open. Dwarf varieties produce sturdier flowers for cutting than the more commonly-grown climbers. Select stems with few open flowers and many well-developed buds. Split stems. Condition in cold water overnight. Carefully wrap the largest buds in tissue paper to keep them from unfolding. Unwrap next morning and petals will spread.

Moss Pink (See Phlox)

MOUNTAIN-BLUET (*Centaurea montana*)

Lasts 4 to 7 days. Cut just after flowers have opened. They are delicate so take care in gathering or petals will be damaged. Split stems. Condition overnight with stems in warm water to start with.

MOUNTAIN FLEECE-FLOWER
(*Polygonum amplexicaule rubrum*)

Cut branches when half in flower. Split woody stems. Remove some leaves: blooms then keep better. Condition overnight with stems in warm water to start with.

Mountain-Laurel (See Laurel)

MULLEIN PINK, ROSE CAMPION, OR
DUSTY MILLER (*Lychnis Coronaria*)

Lasts 4 to 6 days. Cut when 2 or 3 flowers are completely open on each stem. The stem-ends dry almost immediately so recut just before conditioning overnight in warm water to start with.

Musa abyssinica (See Banana)
Muscari botryoides (See Hyacinth, Grape)
Myosotis alpestris (See Forget-me-not)
Narcissus (See Daffodil)

NASTURTIUM (*Tropaeolum majus*)

Flowers last 3 to 5 days; foliage up to 2 weeks. Gather flowers as soon as they have fully opened and also large buds just ready to unfold. *Break* stems away from main stem with forefinger and thumb. Recut and split stems. Condition overnight in cold water. Allow plenty of room for stems to stretch. After they are arranged, flowers turn toward the light and often look lovelier the second day when stems have stretched into a most becoming position. Foliage has character, is versatile. Use it alone, in mixed bouquets, or with its own flowers. Condition for 24 hours, with stems in warm water to start with. Don't let the first wilting dismay you. Most, if not all, the foliage will revive. You can also use the green seed pods to give style to small arrangements.

Nerine sariensis hybrids (See Guernsey Lily)
Nerium Oleander (See Oleander)
Nicotiana (See Flowering Tobacco)
Nigella damascena (See Love-in-a-Mist)
Nymphoea species (See Waterlily)

OAK (*Quercus* in variety)

Foliage is most attractive, especially when forced in early spring. Green acorns are long lasting. Split woody stems. Condition with stems in cold water for about 24 hours. Use colorful autumn foliage with fresh or dried materials. Press foliage for winter use. (See How to Dry Flowers, How to Press.)

Olea ilicifolia (See False Holly)

OLEANDER OR ROSE BAY (*Nerium Oleander*)

Flowers last up to 7 days as florets continue to unfold. Cut clusters when they are about half in flower. A colorless fluid escapes from cut stems. Split stems. Sear them in a flame while you count to 15 slowly. Remove foliage not needed for decoration. Condition overnight with stems in warm water to start with. As a tub plant, Oleander produces quantities of summer flowers. When correctly pruned and given ample light, it blooms again in winter in a greenhouse.

ORANGE BLOSSOMS (*Citrus* in variety)

Lasts 3 to 6 days. Cut flowering branches when one-third to one-half open. Split woody stems. Remove foliage not needed for decoration. Condition overnight with stems in warm water to start with. Submerge non-flowering branches in cold water for about an hour. Remove, split stems, and place in warm water. Let remain until used. Tender foliage that wilts prematurely usually revives in time if stems are cleanly cut and left in water.

ORCHIDS (*Orchidaceae*, Orchid Family)

Some varieties last up to 20 days if cut at proper stage and well-conditioned. Bud unfolds slowly. It takes 3 or 4 days for flower to appear to be fully open, but even then it won't be. Wait another 2 to 3 days before cutting if you want flowers to last well. Cut Orchids prefer a cool, but not too cold, temperature; 48° F. is ideal. Do not store below 48° F.

If possible, keep in an *ice* refrigerator. If Orchids must go into a home electric refrigerator, keep away from freezing coils and wrap flowers first in thin wax paper or cellophane and place in a covered box to prevent drying. Avoid wetting petals. In arrangements, you can keep flowers from becoming water-logged by removing stems from water each day for one-half to three-quarters of an hour. Then put stems back into fresh water. Keep away from drafts and extremes of heat and cold.

Ornamental Eggplant (See Chinese Scarlet Eggplant)
Ornithogalum (See Star-of-Bethlehem)

Osmanthus aquifolium (See False Holly)
Osmunda cinnamomea (See Fern, Cinnamon)
Oswego-Tea (See Bee-Balm)
Oxlip (See Primrose)
Pachysandra terminalis (See Spurge)
Paeonia (See Peony)

PAINTED-TONGUE (*Salpiglossis sinuata, S. hybrida*)

Lasts 4 to 7 days. Cut flowers as soon as they are fully open. Condition overnight with stems in cold water, reaching almost to flower-heads.

Pandanus Veitchii or *P. utilis* (See Screw Pine)

PANSY (*Viola tricolor*)

Lasts 4 to 6 days, longer if lifted with roots. Blossoms last best when pulled, not cut, from plants. Gather when fully open with as much stem and foliage as possible. In this case, as with Chrysanthemums, leaves are an asset. Condition overnight with stems in cold water. If you can spare them, lift entire plants when half in flower. Wash soil from roots; condition overnight with roots in cold water. Cut and conditioned Pansies and Violas last unusually well if stems are inserted in wet sand. Fill a container to within an inch of the top with the sand, and make holes with a pencil to receive the stems. When arrangement is completed, fill container with water so as to cover the sand.

Papaver orientale (See Poppy, Oriental)
Paris Daisy (See Marguerite)

PASSION-FLOWER (*Passiflora caerulea*)

Lasts but 1 day. Cut well-developed buds with petals showing color, in later afternoon. They will be fully open and remain fresh through the next day. Or cut fully-open flowers just before arranging and condition 2 to 4 hours with stems in cold water. Well worth having, if only for the 1 day.

Paulownia tomentosa (See Empress Tree)

PEAR (*Pyrus* in variety)

Lasts 5 to 15 days, but not if blossoms are allowed to open fully on the tree. Then petals drop almost immediately. Cut when only one-quarter of the branch is in flower; buds open nicely in water. Split woody stems. Condition with stems in cold water overnight or until enough blooms are open. Pear blossoms are easily forced into flower any time after Christmas. (See Forcing Flowering Branches.)

Pearlbush (See Spirea)
Pelargonium (See Geranium)
Penny-Flower (See Honesty)
Penstemon (See Beard-Tongue)

PEONY (*Paeonia* in variety)

Lasts 7 to 9 days, or longer under special conditions. Cut peonies from the garden when blooms are less than half open and the sepals (the green covering of the buds) are separated enough to show true color. Store in a cool place, 45° to 50° F., as in a cellar, where blooms may be held up to 3 weeks. Split stem-ends 2 to 3 inches.

Place in cold water and let remain until blooms are sufficiently open. Cut Japanese and single types, including tree peonies, when blooms are about half open. Condition similarly. When exhibiting peonies in a class where fragrance is considered, wrap the whole bouquet of blossoms loosely in thin wax paper or cellophane during conditioning. This holds the fragrance until time for showing. Don't take off stems all the way to the ground. Let at least two sets of leaves remain to help the plant manufacture food which is stored in the roots.

PERILLIA (*Perillia frutescens*)

Insignificant bloom but fruits are good in fresh or dried arrangements, and foliage is excellent. Cut generously all season to make plants branch profusely. Condition overnight with stems in warm water to start with.

PERIWINKLE (*Vinca minor, V. major*)

Flowers last 4 to 5 days. Welcome in early spring for small arrangements. Cut *V. minor* as soon as flowers have fully opened. Let remain overnight with stems in cold water. Wash foliage in cold water to bring out its beauty. Cut *V. major*, the plant used as a ground cover and with larger leaves and blossoms, when flowers are fully open. Condition these flowers and foliage with stems in warm water to start with. Cut stems just below a node and *split* to keep this variety from wilting.

PERIWINKLE, MADAGASCAR (*Vinca rosea*)

Flowers last 3 to 5 days, buds continuing to open for a week or longer. A must for arrangers! Possesses many good qualities, yet is relatively unknown. The foliage alone makes a pretty, shining-green bouquet. Cut when 2 or 3 flowers on each stem are fully open. All buds showing color will open fully. Split stems. They will be woody late in the season. Condition overnight in cold water. Remove some of the upper foliage to show flowers to better advantage and help them last longer. Remove blossoms as they wither. The newly-opened ones will make a fresh bouquet.

Persian Buttercup (See Ranunculus)

PERUVIAN DAFFODIL OR TIGER-FLOWER
(*Tigridia Pavonia*)

Each flower lasts but 1 day. Recut stems under water after removing fully-opened flowers from plants. Condition 1 to 2 hours.

PERUVIAN LILY (*Alstroemeria* in variety)

Clusters last up to 5 days. A wiry, sturdy stem supports the flowers. Cut when slightly more than half the buds are fully open in each cluster. Split stems. Condition overnight in cold water reaching almost to flower-heads.

PETUNIA (*Petunia hybrida*)

Lasts 4 to 7 days. Cut flowers when fully open, or nearly so, and shape plants to outside buds and breaks. Then you will have plenty of bloom. Flowers and foliage collapse after cutting but revive if conditioned overnight in 5 per cent sugar solution. Use 4 level teaspoons to each quart of water. Foliage decays rapidly in water so be sure to strip stems below water-level and as far above as looks well. Petals fall easily from their sheaths so handle carefully. (When growing all-double and ruffled petunias from seed, do not discard weak seedlings. These usually produce most shapely flowers in the best colors.)

Philadelphus coronarius (See Mockorange)

PHILODENDRON (*Philodendron* in variety)

Rarely wilts, requires little care, roots in water, and is fine with cut flowers or with driftwood. Cut stems just below a node. Remove foliage below water-level, although foliage does survive submerging longer than that of most other plants. Wipe or spray foliage to keep it free of dust.

PHLOX (*Phlox* in variety)

Lasts 7 to 12 days. Cut when clusters are one-quarter to one-half open. Split stems. Condition overnight with stems in cold water or until sufficiently open. Cutting the first blooms encourages a second flowering later in the season. Sometimes Phlox drops florets prematurely. This is due to selection of blooms past their prime, improper conditioning, or lack of humidity.

Phoradendron flavescens (See Mistletoe)
Physalis Alkekengi or *P. Bunyardi* (See Chinese Lantern-Plant)

PIERIS (*Pieris* or *Andromeda japonica*)

Flowers last up to 10 days, foliage also enduring. Cut when clusters are about half open. Condition in cold water overnight or until flowers have sufficiently opened. Foliage is perfect for cutting at any time of year. If growth is new, submerge for 1 hour. Then split woody stems and keep in cold water until used.

Pincushion-Flower (See *Scabiosa*)

PINE AND PINE CONES (*Pinus* in variety)

Both excellent keepers. Wash branches and strip off needles on stems below water-line. (See also Evergreens.) Pine is easily bent into desired curves. (See Plate 4.) When brought into a warm room, cones pop open, expelling seeds. Expanded cones are attractive, but if you don't wish them to open, collect when tightly closed and coat with clear shellac or plastic spray.

PINEAPPLE (*Ananas sativus*)

Just for fun, root the leaves from the top of a fresh pineapple. To do this, cut top off just above the fruit. Insert base of this leaf cluster into moist sand. It will root and put forth new green leaves. Green tops last well and can be interesting with fresh flowers, succulents, fruits, and vegetables. Dry the tops for winter use.

Pinks (See Carnation)

PITCHER-PLANT (*Sarracenia* in variety)

Lasts 7 to 10 days. Cut flowers when fully open. Exotic leaves are hollow, forming pitchers with lids.

Select the size foliage best suited to your design. Submerge flowers and foliage about half an hour or until they are firm and crisp. Then split stems and condition overnight in cold water.

PLANTAIN-LILY OR FUNKIA (*Hosta* in variety)

Florets last 2 to 3 days, spikes go on opening up to 7 days. Cut when 2 or 3 basal flowers are open. Split stems. Condition overnight in cold water reaching almost to flower-heads. Good curves result when stems are placed slantwise in container. Buds open well in water. *H. subcordata grandiflora* is fragrant.

Platycodon grandiflora (See Chinese Balloon-Flower)

PLUM (*Prunus domestica*)

Flowering branches continue to open for 10 days. Cut when about one-quarter of the blossoms on a branch are open. Split woody stems. Condition in cold water overnight or until sufficiently open for arranging. Fine for early spring. (See Forcing Flowering Branches.)

PLUME-POPPY (*Bocconia* or *Macleaya cordata*)

Lasts 3 to 5 days. Cut flower panicles when they are slightly less than half open. Split stems. Check the flow of yellowish juice by searing ends in a flame for 15 seconds. Then condition in cold water overnight. Remove most of the large leaves so as to show flower-heads to advantage. This dries well for winter use. Cut panicles when three-fourths to fully open. Remove leaves and hang to dry. It's a good idea, even when drying, to sear stems and condition flowers until they appear fresh and turgid. Then they won't wilt before you bunch and hang them, and results will be more satisfying.

Plumeria (See Frangipani)
Poa (See Blue Lyme Grass)
Podophyllum peltatum (See May Apple)

POINSETTIA (*Euphorbia pulcherrima*)

Lasts 4 to 5 days. Immediately after cutting, put stem-ends in boiling water for 1½ to 3 minutes. Or sear stem-ends by holding in a flame while you count to 15 slowly. After either treatment, condition stems in cold water overnight or for at least 8 hours. (It has been suggested that flowers last longer if a handful of rock salt is added to each 2 quarts of water. I have not tried this. You may wish to experiment.)

Polianthes tuberosa (See Tuberose)
Polygonum amplexicaule rubrum (See Mountain Fleece-Flower)
Poor-Mans-Orchid (See Butterfly-Flower)

POPPY, CALIFORNIA (*Eschscholzia californica*)

Lasts 4 to 6 days. Flowers close toward late afternoon without detracting from their beauty or keeping quality. They open again next day. If you have enough plants, lift with roots attached. This gives longer stems and better water-conduction. Or cut buds when petals are about as long as they will be when flowers are fully open. Condition overnight with stems or roots in cold water.

Plate 5

Submerge 1 to 2 inches
of stem-end in boiling water
2 to 3 minutes.

or...

Split stem —
sear 15 seconds.

POPPY, ORIENTAL (*Papaver orientale*)

Contrary to popular belief, flowers last 4 to 5 days. Gather in advanced-bud stage, when petals are well formed, cupped, and ready to unfold. It is questionable whether tight buds will open. Sear stem-ends immediately, holding them in a flame while you count to 15 slowly. Sear stems at length to be used in final arrangement. Then condition in deep cold water overnight or for at least 8 hours.

A little melted candle wax, same color as petals, dropped inside each blossom at base of petals delays shattering. Do this after stems have been in water for a time and have opened sufficiently to permit easy access to blossoms.

PORTULACA OR ROSE-MOSS
(*Portulaca grandiflora*)

Flowers and buds last 3 to 6 days. Rarely used as a cut flower because it closes toward late afternoon. When cutting, avoid crushing the soft, fleshy stems. Try lifting whole plants and arranging them in low bowls. They are effective this way, especially the doubles whose buds are so beautiful. Condition overnight with stems or roots in cold water.

PRIMROSE (*Primula* in variety)

Lasts 5 to 8 days, depending on variety. Cut when clusters are one-half to three-quarters open. Try not to bruise stems. Split and condition overnight with stems in warm water to start with. Occasionally a return to warm water is necessary to bring flowers to perfection.

Princess Feather (See Cockscomb)

PRIVET (*Ligustrum* in variety)

Most of us are so tired of the common privet that we neglect the elegant, lesser-known Glossy Privet (*L. Lucidum*) and Chinese Privet (*L. sinensis*) with handsome foliage, flowers, and fruits. Cut when panicles are one-quarter to one-half open. Cut foliage at any time, but avoid young, tender growth which may prove difficult to condition. Cut fruits when they are mature. Treat flowers, foliage, and fruits as woody material. Split stems. Condition overnight with stems in cold water. Fruits of *L. vulgare* dry well for winter use. If necessary, spray with clear plastic to prevent shriveling and dropping.

Prunus domestica (See Plum)
Prunus (See Cherry Blossoms)

PURPLE LOOSESTRIFE (*Lythrum Salicaria*)

Lasts 4 to 7 days. Cut when one-quarter or less of the lower florets are open. Remove foliage not necessary for decoration. Condition overnight with stems in warm water to start with. This is an exceptional keeper when cut at the proper stage. If cut too late, petals fall almost immediately.

PUSSYWILLOW (*Salix discolor*)

Bring indoors for forcing as soon as buds begin to swell. Or cut when one-quarter to one-half the branch has reached maturity. Split stems and condition in cold water. This also keeps well without water, but some buds drop, and, of course, flowers do not open.

Pyracantha coccinea (See Firethorn)
Pyrus (See Pear)

QUEEN-ANNES-LACE (*Daucus carota*)

Lasts 7 to 12 days. This wildling enchants us with its delicate beauty. Use it in bud, full bloom, fresh, dried, or pressed for decorations under glass or in pictures. Take at any stage, but it keeps particularly well if cut before it is completely open. Condition overnight with stems in cold water reaching almost to flower-heads. Avoid wetting flowers. For drying, cut at various stages: light-green in early summer, reddish-bronze in autumn. Hang to dry. For pressing, gather when completely open. Then either cut flowers from stems or leave stems attached, depending on future use. Press between sheets of weighted newspaper. Protect blossoms on both sides with pieces of tissue paper. It takes 2 to 4 weeks for drying.

QUINCE, FLOWERING (*Cydonia japonica*)

Flowers continue to open up to 2 weeks and appear mostly before foliage. Cut when approximately one-quarter or less of the buds are fully open on a branch. Buds open well indoors. Split woody stems. Condition overnight with stems in cold water. Excellent for forcing in late winter. (See Forcing Flowering Branches.)

Rabbits-Foot Clover (See Clover)
Ranunculus (See Buttercup, Wild, also below)

RANUNCULUS, TURBAN OR
PERSIAN BUTTERCUP (*Ranunculus asiaticus*)

Lasts 6 to 12 days. One of the finest flowers for cutting. Gather when about three-quarters open. If allowed to open completely before cutting, flowers are slightly larger but do not last as long. Well-developed buds unfold in water, though flowers are somewhat smaller. Split stems. Condition overnight in cold water reaching almost to flower-heads. Stems will curve if placed slant-wise in the container while conditioning. Recut and split stems of Ranunculus from the florist. Recondition with stems in deep water for at least 3 hours before arranging.

RATTLEBOX (*Crotalaria retusa*)

Lasts 5 to 7 days. Gather when one-half to three-quarters of the flowering spike is open, but before lowest florets begin to fade. Spike should be fairly well developed as buds do not open well indoors. Condition overnight with stems in cold water. Spikes sometimes grow with pleasing curves. To achieve them, place some stems slantwise in the conditioning container so tips will turn upward. Cut central stalks of plants first. Side shoots will then develop and continue flowering until frost.

REDBUD (*Cercis canadensis*)

Opens over a period of 4 to 5 days. Flowers appear before foliage. Cut budded branches before flowers open. Flowers drop quickly if cut *after* they have opened outdoors. Split woody stems. Put stems in hot water, 80° to 100° F. Spray branches with a fine mist of cold water once daily to prevent dropping of buds and to encourage them to open.

Red Hot Poker-Plant (See Torch-Lily)
Reseda odorata (See Mignonette)

RHODODENDRON (*Rhododendron* in variety)

Flowers last 7 to 10 days and are superior for cutting. Take when one-half or less of the florets are open in each cluster. Submerge flowers and stems in cold water until petals are crisp, ½ to 2 hours, depending on conditions at the start. Then split stems at base. Condition in cold water overnight or until used. Besides the large-leaved type, there are also small-leaved varieties with evergreen foliage which lasts well and is interesting for all-green arrangements. Submerge young, new foliage as you do the flowers.

Rhus glabra (See Sumac)
Ricinus communis (See Castor-Bean)
Rocket Larkspur (See Larkspur)

ROSE (*Rosa* in variety)

Cut with very sharp rose or pruning shears in a way not to damage plants. (Stems may be recut later with a sharp knife.) Avoid taking too much foliage from plants, particularly the first year, or you will have weak, undernourished growth. Cut stems diagonally about ¼ inch above a leaf, letting at least 2 well-developed leaves remain between the cut and the point where the flower-stem joins the main stem. The 2 remaining eyes will develop into new shoots. The top eye should be on the outside of the stem. Then the new shoot will branch outward. (Eyes on the inside of a stem grow inward, crowding the center of a bush.)

The best time to cut Roses is toward the last hours of daylight. Remove foliage from the base of stems. Split stems. Condition overnight with stems in cold water reach-

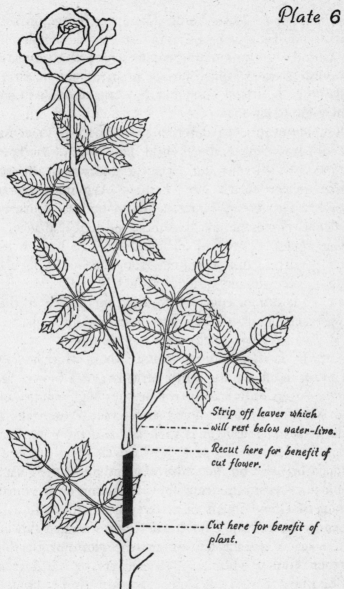

Plate 6

Strip off leaves which
will rest below water-line.

Recut here for benefit of
cut flower.

Cut here for benefit of
plant.

ing almost up to flower-heads. The upper foliage of most Roses is not damaged by being in water for this conditioning period. Add one of the commercial preservatives, if you wish, at the specified rate or prepare your own formula (page 24). Roses keep best in water which has been adjusted to pH 4.

Keeping qualities of different types of Roses vary. All do not last as long as the Hybrid Teas which have been bred to last well when cut. Even these vary with variety. These are particularly good keepers: Auguste Viktoria, Charlotte Armstrong, Crimson Glory, Eclipse, Etoile de Hollande, Peace, Picture, Radiance, and Red Radiance.

Cut *Hybrid Teas* with distinctly pointed buds when outer petals are just separating from the bud. Globular buds of very double varieties should be a little further open. Your aim, of course, is to bring the flowers to that most beautiful stage when they are about three-quarters open. (This is always a challenge to exhibitors.)

Cut *Floribundas* and other cluster Roses, which usually do not open all at once, when perhaps 1 or 2 blooms are three-quarters open and the rest are just beginning to unfold. Most of the buds should show color. Again take as little stem and foliage as possible so as to promote more bloom.

Cut *Climbers* and *Pillar Roses* according to their habit of bloom. Avoid sacrificing next year's crop on the once-bloomers. Of course, if plants are large and well-established, it won't matter how many long-stemmed flowers you take. Abundant flowers are the glory of the big climber. Gather when 2 or 3 petals are separated from the bud.

Cabbage, China, Damask, French, and other "old-fashioned" Roses do not, in most cases, last very well when cut. They seem to burst into bloom rather than unfold slowly. Cut the singles and semidoubles in the advanced-bud stage, when 2 or 3 outer petals have separated. Let the very double types open a little further before you cut them.

With *Florist's Roses*, unpack immediately. Remove any bruised petals or crushed foliage. Cut about 1 inch off base of stems. Recondition with stems in cold water for at least 3 hours before arranging. If the Roses have lost a great deal of moisture in transit and arrive rather wilted and soft (an unusual condition now that they are successfully flown even overseas), you can revive them quickly. Just recut stems, split, and place in water as warm as your hand will bear.

For exhibiting, you can keep Roses in good condition for about 1 week beforehand. Cut each type as suggested above. Place stems immediately in cold water. Insert in the center of the container a thin stick or reed long enough to reach several inches above the tallest bloom. This will prevent pressure against Roses from the covering placed around them—which is the next step. To keep out air, pull a moisture- and vaporproof plastic bag over Roses and down over top of container. Blooms may first be wrapped with Saran Wrap or thin wax paper, but let the stems extend well into the water. Then secure the outer plastic covering with rubber bands, string, or tape pulled around the opening of the container. Or, reverse the business and place the container down in the bottom of a large plastic bag; then close it at the top. Next, place container with Roses in a refrigerator. A temperature of about 34° F. is best. Inspect from time to time to see if excess moisture, which will discolor blooms, has collected inside the wrapping. If flowers appear unduly moist, provide a fresh, dry wrapping.

If you must cut during a dry spell, condition before refrigerating with stems in cold water right up to the necks of the Roses for several hours—until the Roses appear normally turgid. And you would do well to soak the roots beforehand for some hours with a slow-running hose on the bed.

Because of unseasonal weather or when you have a choice bud with perfect stem and foliage it is sometimes necessary to keep Hybrid Teas longer than 10 days. Then the method known as "dry packaging" is employed: Cut Roses pretty much in bud with just 1 or 2 outer petals loosening. Roses should be of normal turgidity when gathered. Without putting stems in water, place blooms in a moisture- and vaporproof container, seal with as little air left in package as possible, and place in a refrigerator. Store Roses upright (without water) in a suitable container with weight resting on stem-ends, or horizontally without crushing or crowding. The best temperature is 32° F.; below 31° F. there is likely to be deterioration. Precise and accurate temperature control is important as is good air circulation during storage. Special cardboard boxes, paraffin-lined, are available for this dry-pack method. If you use it, overwrap boxes with a moisture- and vaporproof material. A simulated container of aluminum foil or plastic may be used. To remove excess air from a plastic bag or other covering before closing it, place the mouth of the Rose-filled bag over the suction nozzle of an ordinary home vacuum-cleaner. The reason for withdrawing surplus air surrounding Roses is that if left in quantity it absorbs some moisture from the Roses. In this manner it is possible to keep the flowers for more than 30 days.

When you remove Roses from the refrigerator, cut 1 inch off the stems diagonally, with a sharp knife. Immediately place stems in water as warm as your hand will stand comfortably. Let remain for several hours or even a day, depending on temperatures. Flowers unfold leisurely in a cool place; more quickly where it is warm. The longer a Rose is refrigerated, the faster the bud will open after exposure to ordinary room temperatures. Doubles open more slowly than varieties with fewer petals and one variety may open faster than another. Thus, very double Roses, like Peace, open more slowly than the semidouble Scorcher or the single Dainty Bess.

Rose Bay (See Oleander)
Rose Campion (See Mullein Pink)

ROSE-MALLOW (*Hibiscus Moscheutos* or *H. palustris*)

Lasts only 1 or 2 days. Cut in advanced-bud stage. Let stems remain in cold water while buds open. Not long enduring after fully blown.

ROSEMARY (*Rosmarinus officinalis*)

The gray-green foliage, almost evergreen, lasts up to 2 weeks, blends well with many flowers. Cut at any time, but avoid taking very young growth as it is difficult to condition. Split woody stems. Condition overnight with stems in cold water. It is unusual for Rosemary to wilt prematurely, but it may if plants are grown in rich soil. Revive by placing stems in hot water, 80° to 100° F. If 1 to 2 inches of the stem-tips bend when you don't want them to, remove from water, let foliage wilt slightly, and put again into the hot water. Or allow branches to wilt slightly immediately after cutting and before you condition them. If you do this, recut stems before placing them in water. Rosemary is easily bent into desired curves with warm hands.

Rose-Moss (See Portulaca)
Rose-of-Sharon (See Althea)
Rudbeckia hirta (See Black-eyed Susan)

RUE OR HERB-OF-GRACE (*Ruta graveolens*)

Flowers last 5 to 7 days, foliage up to 12 days. Cut when clusters have 3 to 6 fully-opened flowers. Take foliage at any stage, shaping plants as you cut. Split stems. Condition overnight with stems in hot water, 80° to 100° F., to start with. Collect fruits while green or later in fall when they turn tan. These need no conditioning, unless stems are soft and contain a fair amount of moisture. Dry fruits for winter use.

Rumex (See Dock)
Ruta graveolens (See Rue)

SAGE (*Salvia* in variety)

Flowers last 5 to 10 days, depending on variety. Garden sage (*S. officinalis*), we know as an herb for seasoning, but the rough-textured gray leaves are wonderfully decorative. Cut well-developed foliage any time. Cut flowers when one-quarter to one-half the spike is open. Split woody stems. Condition overnight with stems in warm water to start with.

Blue Salvia (*S. farinaceae*) has a whitish "bloom" on stems and buds, as if dusted with talcum, but it doesn't rub off. Excellent fresh or dried. Cut when lower half of flowering spike has opened. Condition overnight in warm water to start with, and with some stems slantwise in the container so they will curve.

Gentian Sage (*S. patens*) and Scarlet Sage (*S. splendens*) should be cut when one-half to three-quarters of the spike is open. Split stems. Condition overnight with stems in warm water to start with. As red varieties of *S. splendens* drop petals, red bracts remain along the stems. When these feel papery in texture, cut for winter use.

SAINT JOHNSWORT (*Hypericum* in variety)

Lasts 3 to 5 days. Let blooms open fully before cutting. Split stems. Condition overnight in cold water. Tight buds, although decorative, do not open well in water.

Saintpaulia ionantha (See African Violet)
Salix discolor (See Pussywillow)
Salpiglossis (See Painted-Tongue)
Salvia (Sec Sage)
Sansevieria zeylanica (See Snake-Plant)
Sarracenia (See Pitcher-Plant)
Satin-Flower (See also Honesty)

SATIN-FLOWER (*Godetia* in variety)

Lasts 2 to 5 days. Lift plants of the dwarf variety as you do with Pansy, Sweet Alyssum, and other small growers. Wash soil from roots; trim away excess foliage and buds. Condition overnight with roots in cold water. With *G. amoena*, which grows to 1 to 2 feet, cut when flowers are three-quarters to fully open. Split stems. Condition overnight in cold water.

SCABIOSA, PINCUSHION-FLOWER OR
SWEET SCABIOSA (*Scabiosa atropurpurea*)

Lasts 4 to 8 days. Cut when almost fully open. Buds are interesting, darker than flowers, and open somewhat in water, but must be well developed to open completely after they are cut. Split stems. Remove foliage. Condition overnight with stems in cold water reaching almost to flower-heads. When petals fall, an unusual green, immature seed pod remains which can be used effectively. Late in season, collect seed pods to dry for winter bouquets.

SCARLET PLUME (*Euphorbia fulgens*)

Lasts 5 to 9 days. Cut flowering branches that are one-half to three-quarters open. Split and sear ends of stems by holding them in a flame while you count to 15 slowly. Condition stems overnight in cold water. Remove some leaves close to flowers so they will show better and also to extend their life. If a milky juice escapes as you remove leaves, submerge stems in cold water for a moment or two to cleanse them. This is usually greenhouse grown and available around Christmas and through late winter.

Scarlet Sage (See Sage)
Schizanthus pinnatus (See Butterfly-Flower)

SCOTCH-BROOM (*Cytisus scoparius*)

Foliage lasts 2 to 3 weeks. Good for line arrangements and easily bent into curves. Cut branches of desired length and clean by swishing around in cold water a few minutes. Split woody stems. Condition in cold water until used. Branches may be tied into desired forms and submerged in cold water until the new lines are fixed. Remove and, while still tied, condition stems in water. Let dry before untieing. Foliage lasts well, but blossoms do not. Seed pods are fine to dry for winter use. (Some of the mixed hybrids have more durable blossoms but must be chosen with care for northern gardens as they are doubtfully hardy.)

SCREW-PINE (*Pandanus* in variety)

Foliage lasts for weeks. When leaves have attained size desired, cut at point where they join the main stem. Cleanse foliage and condition overnight with stems in cold water.

SEA-LAVENDER (*Limonium latifolium*)

Flowers last 5 to 10 days. To use fresh, cut when clusters are half in flower. Condition overnight with stems in cold water. For drying, cut when one-half to three-quarters open. Hang in the usual manner.

SEA-PINK OR THRIFT (*Armeria maritima*)

Lasts 5 to 7 days. Cut when globelike flower-heads are half open. They open completely in water. Condition overnight with stems in cold water reaching almost to flower-heads. Stems assume interesting curves when placed slantwise in container during conditioning. Curves are more pronounced when flowers are allowed to wilt slightly before conditioning.

SEDUM (*Sedum spectabile*)

Flowers last 7 to 10 days, foliage 2 to 3 weeks. Cut when clusters are half in flower; they continue opening in water. Condition overnight with stems in cold water. You can use foliage of varieties with dense, close-growing leaves successfully without water, but submerge first for 20 to 30 minutes.

Sempervivums (See Houseleeks)

SHADBUSH (*Amelanchier canadensis*)

Lasts 5 to 7 days. Flowers precede foliage. Cut when not more than half the flowers are open on the branch. Split woody stems. Condition overnight with stems in cold water.

Shell-Flower (See Bells-of-Ireland)
Silverod (See Goldenrod)

SKUNK CABBAGE (*Symplocarpus foetidus*)

Flowers last 8 to 12 days. Gather flowers when they are formed and large enough to show, leaves when they are the size you want for your design. You can get rid of the unpleasant odor of the flowers by removing stamens and submerging blooms in ice-water for about 1 hour. Then keep stems in cold water until used. Flowers take interesting forms as they dry and curl. They may be completely dried for winter use.

SLIPPERWORT (*Calceolaria hybrida*)

Lasts 3 to 5 days. Cut flowers when about half the blooms are open in each cluster. Split stems. Condition overnight with stems in warm water to start with. Avoid wetting flower petals. Foliage is too perishable to use.

SNAKE-PLANT OR BOWSTRING-HEMP
(*Sansevieria zeylanica*)

Flowers appear irregularly and are so short lived they are not worth cutting. Leaves are practically indestructible when cut. I have had them last 4 to 6 weeks out of water! Cleanse well before arranging. A wad of wet cotton works fine. When they are dry, rub a very small amount of olive oil over the leaves to make them shine. Condition at first for about 8 hours with stems in 2 to 3 inches of cold water. Then arrange with or without water. (If leaves are still fresh when arrangement has served its purpose, 3 or 4 inches of the tips may be cut off and propagated.) Although they are naturally rigid, leaves can be gently curved and twisted with warm hands.

SNAPDRAGON (*Antirrhinum majus*)

Lasts 5 to 12 days. When gathering from your garden, cut when spikes are half in flower. Condition overnight, or for at least 8 hours, with stems in water adjusted to pH 4. Use one of the commercial preservatives or the home-formula with hot water, 80° to 100° F., to start with. (See page 24.) For curving stems place some slantwise during conditioning. For very straight stems, use deep, upright containers.

Another way to condition Snapdragons is to submerge flowering stems in cold water with no preservative added. Remove when flowers and foliage are crisp, after about half an hour. Gently shake off excess water. Then condition stems in solution as above. This method makes flowers last unusually well but it destroys some of the fragrance. As it becomes necessary, pinch off carefully or cut off with a pointed scissors the faded florets from the lower stems. Recut stems of Snapdragons from the florist and recondition for at least 3 to 4 hours before arranging.

SNOW-ON-THE-MOUNTAIN
(*Euphorbia marginata*)

Foliage lasts up to 1 week. Grown for its attractive light-green, white, or variegated leaves. Flowers are insignificant. Check flow of milky juice in stems with boiling-water treatment or searing in a flame.

Solanum Pseudo-Capsicum (See Jerusalem-Cherry)
Solidago (See Goldenrod)
Sorrel (See Dock)
Southernwood (See Artemesia)
Spanish Bluebell (See Squill)

SPEEDWELL (*Veronica* in variety)

Lasts 4 to 6 days. Cut when spikes are half, or slightly less than half, in flower; buds will open in water. Condition overnight with stems in warm water at the start. Place some slantwise so as to make them curve.

SPICE-BUSH (*Benzoin aestivale*)

Flowers open over a period of 10 to 12 days. Bark is fragrant when crushed. Cut in advanced-bud stage. Split woody stems. Condition overnight with stems in cold water. Nice for forcing. (See Forcing Flowering Branches.)

SPIDER-FLOWER (*Cleome spinosa*)

Lasts 4 to 5 days. Cut when clusters are about half in flower. Wilts when cut even though placed immediately in water, but revives quickly. Split stems. Condition overnight with stems in warm water to start with.

SPIREA (*Spirea* in variety)

Lasts 4 to 10 days, depending on variety. Cut flowers from shrubby sorts when one-fourth to one-half the branch is in bloom. Split woody stems. Condition overnight, or until flowers are sufficiently open, with stems in warm water to start with. For forcing into flower in late winter or early spring, cut when buds begin to swell. (See Forcing Flowering Branches.)

Hardhack or Steeplebush (*S. tomentosa*) is excellent for drying. Cut when fully open. Hang to dry in the usual manner. (Don't confuse Spirea with Astilbe, an herbaceous perennial; see also Astilbe.)

SPURGE (*Pachysandra terminalis*)

Lasts indefinitely when cut, even roots in water. Cut foliage when fully developed; flowers are fragrant but insignificant. Cleanse leaves in cold water. Condition overnight with stems in cold water. Foliage is excellent with many flowers, also with fruits and vegetables.

SPURGE, FLOWERING (*Euphorbia corollata*)

Flowers last up to 1 week. Cut clusters when half in flower. Recut and split stems just before placing in hot water, 80° to 100° F., to check flow of milky juice. Let stems remain in water overnight to condition. Searing is unnecessary. In fact, sometimes I have had luck conditioning stems just in cold water. (This is a lovely substitute for Babys-Breath.)

SQUILL OR SPANISH BLUEBELL
(*Scilla* in variety)

Lasts 5 to 8 days. *Scilla campanulata*, also *S. sibirica* and *S. autumnalis*, should all be cut when half the flowers are fully open along the spike. Split stems. Condition overnight in deep cold water with some stems placed slantwise to make them curve.

SQUIRREL-TAIL GRASS (*Hordeum jubatum*)

Grown mainly for ornamental fruits. Gather these when *nearly* ripe, when ripe, and in between to obtain varying shades of color. Or use fruits green in fresh arrangements. Cut ripe fruits for winter use and hang to dry. For fresh arrangements, cut some of the young growth and condition with stems in cold water overnight.

Stachys lanata (See Woolly Lambs-Ear)

STAR-OF-BETHLEHEM
(*Ornithogalum umbellatum, O. arabicum*)

Lasts 5 to 8 days. Cut stems above the basal white portion when flower clusters are half open. Condition overnight with stems in cold water. Stems are rather weak so flowers incline to droop. Use this trait to advantage when arranging. Flowers seem to last longer when 6 to 8 stems are bound together with a Twistem. This also holds stems straighter.

STATICE (*Limonium* or *Statice sinuatum*)

An "everlasting" in water or dried. Condition fresh flowers a few hours with stems in cold water. For either use, cut when flowers are fully open. One of the best for drying; keeps its color and good form.

Steeplebush (See Spirea)

STEPHANOTIS OR MADAGASCAR JASMINE (*Stephanotis floribunda*)

Lasts 4 to 6 days. The florist usually offers flowers with very short stems, and these are rather soft. For arranging, order with longer stems, which will then be somewhat woody. Latex, a rubbery fluid, exudes from cut stems so split them to aid dispersion and sear stem-ends in a flame for 15 seconds. Then place immediately in cold water to condition overnight. Remove foliage not needed for decoration. You can capture the delightful fragrance by wrapping your bouquet loosely in cellophane or thin wax paper until displayed.

STOCK OR GILLIFLOWER (*Mathiola incana*)

Flowers last 5 to 12 days, depending on variety. Singles do not last as well as doubles. Cut flowering spike when one-fourth to one-half open, but *before* florets at base begin to fade. Split woody stems for 3 to 4 inches, depending on length. Condition overnight with stems in *very cold water* to begin with. A fine mist of cold water sprayed on flowers and foliage keeps them fresh longer, encourages buds to open. Experiments at the University of Illinois indicate that Stock keeps best when water is adjusted to pH 4. Three heaping teaspoons of sugar and 2 tablespoons of white distilled vinegar added to 1 quart of water lowers the pH from 7 to 4. But you should first test pH of water to be used. If it is other than 7, this formula should be varied.

Stock may wilt prematurely, but, when stems are recut, split, and held in boiling water for 1½ to 3 minutes, and then conditioned in cold water, it revives. Usually it stays fresh until nearly all the buds open.

Stonecrop (See Sedum)

STRAWBERRY OR SWEET-SHRUB OR CAROLINA ALLSPICE (*Calycanthus fertilis*)

Flowers last 5 to 8 days. Cut branches when one-quarter to one-half the flowers are open. Split woody stems. Condition overnight with stems in cold water. Remove some of the foliage along stem to show flowers to better advantage. Flowers release a spicy fragrance when crushed.

Strelitzia Reginae (See Bird-of-Paradise-Flower)

SUMAC (*Rhus* in variety)

Flowers last 5 to 8 days. *Rhus javanica* and *R. glabra* have showy flower panicles, excellent for large arrangements, but fall foliage and the scarlet fruits are also widely used. Cut flowers when panicles are about half open. Remove foliage not necessary for decoration. Condition overnight with stems in cold water. Cut fruits for fresh or dried arrangements whenever you find the coloring you want. Fruits become more vivid as season advances. Treat same as flowers. For drying, collect fruits at the height of their color (usually late summer), place stems upright in containers without water, or store in open boxes until used.

Summer Forget-Me-Not (See Alkanet)

SUNFLOWER (*Helianthus* in variety)

Lasts 6 to 10 days. Cut when petals are turned back but centers tight. Where more than one blossom tops the stem, take when clusters are at least half open. Remove leaves not necessary for decoration. Split stems. Condition overnight with stems in warm water, 80° to 100° F., to start with. Stems of the Annual Sunflower are often unable to support the massive flower-heads. When cut, these can be strengthened by inserting a heavy wire through the center of the stem into the calyx. This variety is interesting when dried. Let some flowers go to seed and dry on the plants; then gather. They are attractive even after seeds have fallen or are removed.

SWEET ALYSSUM
   (*Alyssum* or *Lobularia maritimum*)

Lasts 5 to 8 days. Cut individual stems when half in bloom. Buds will open in water and stems lengthen somewhat. You can also lift small plants when about half in flower. Condition overnight with stems or roots in cold water. Delightfully fragrant.

SWEET PEA (*Lathyrus* in variety)

Lasts 5 to 8 days. When only the tip of the flowering stem remains in bud, gather annual type by gently breaking off slender stems with thumb and forefinger. Cut Perennial Sweet Pea when clusters are about half in flower. Recut stems under water at the length they are to be used in final arrangement. Condition overnight with stems in a 5 per cent solution of sugar using warm water—about 4 teaspoons to 1 quart of water. Avoid wetting flower petals.

SWEET ROCKET (*Hesperis matronalis*)

Lasts 5 to 9 days. Cut when one-quarter to one-half the flowers are open in each cluster. Condition overnight with stems in warm water to start with. You can get long stems from established plants. To make stems curve, place some slantwise in container during conditioning. (This is one advantage of Sweet Rocket over Phlox whose sturdy, stiff stems refuse to curve.)

Sweet-Shrub (See Strawberry Shrub)

SWEET WILLIAM (*Dianthus barbatus*)

Lasts 1 to 2 weeks. Cut when clusters are half in flower. Buds open well after cutting. Split stems. Condition with stems in cold water overnight, or until enough buds open. Indoors in water, buds open more slowly than when they are left in the garden, especially if weather is very hot and dry. Since Sweet William lasts a long time, watch stems and recut if they decay.

SWEET WIVELSFIELD (*Dianthus carthusianorum*)

Cut and treat same as Sweet William.

Symplocarpus foetidus (See Skunk Cabbage)
Syringa (See Lilac)
Tagetes (See Marigold)
Tanacetum vulgare (See Tansy)

TANSY (*Tanacetum vulgare*)

Lasts 1 to 2 weeks. Excellent for fresh or dried bouquets. For either purpose, cut when blossoms are almost fully open. Buds do not open after cutting. Condition overnight with stems in cold water. When dried, flower-heads shrink considerably, so collect generous quantities.

Taraxacum officinale (See Dandelion)

TASSEL-FLOWER (*Cacalia* or *Emilia sagittata*)

Cut stems topped by a few fully-opened flowers. Split stems. Strip foliage not necessary for decoration. Condition overnight in cold water reaching almost to flower-heads.

TEAZLE OR FULLERWEED (*Dipsacus sylvestris*)

Lasts 5 to 8 days. Condition blossoms overnight with stems in cold water. They are of less interest than fruits, which are gathered for winter use. Wear gloves and remove thorns from base of stems at time of cutting to facilitate future handling. Collect at various stages: green in midsummer, tan in late summer, dark-brown in fall. Also gather various sizes—small, medium, and large fruits. Look for stems with interesting curves and angles. Green stems are somewhat soft so hang upside-down to dry. Tan and brown fruits usually have stiff stems and may be placed directly in open boxes or upright containers, without water, until used. Spray at Christmas, or for other holidays, with silver, gold, colored, or clear enamel spray; sprinkle while wet with artificial snow or colorful sequins.

Thalictrum (See Meadow-Rue)

THERMOPSIS (*Thermopsis caroliniana*)

Lasts 7 to 12 days. Cut in early stages when one-third to one-half the flowering spike is open. Split stems. Condition overnight in cold water. (Even though stems are hollow, use cold water for conditioning as warm or hot water causes quick deterioration.) Place slantwise in container during conditioning; stems will curve slightly.

THISTLE (*Cirsium* in variety)

Rarely used in fresh bouquets. For drying, cut (wear gloves) when about three-quarters open and hang upside-down to dry. Spray with clear plastic if there is any sign of shattering. Flowers retain their delicate lavender color when properly dried.

Thrift (See Sea-Pink)
Tiger-Flower (See Peruvian Daffodil)
Tigridia Pavonia (See Peruvian Daffodil)
Tithonia (See Mexican Sunflower)

TORCH-LILY OR RED HOT POKER-PLANT
(*Kniphofia hybrida*)

Lasts up to 1 week. Cut when one-quarter to one-third the flowering spike is open, unless the green-shaded buds are wanted for a definite color scheme. Split stems. Condition overnight with stems in cold water. You can easily bend the stiff stems into graceful curves with warm hands, or place stems slantwise in container during conditioning. After being arranged, stems take up a lot of water. Be careful to replenish water and recut stems as required.

Torenia Fournieri (See Wishbone-Flower)
Trachymene caerulea (See Blue Lace-Flower)
Transvaal Daisy (See Gerbera)

TREE-MALLOW (*Lavatera trimestris*)

Continues to open for 5 to 7 days. Cut when 1 or 2 flowers in each cluster are fully open. Buds will develop into full-blown flowers indoors. Split stems. Condition overnight with stems in cold water.

Trifolium (See Clover)
Thrift (See Sea-Pink)
Triticum aestivum (See Wheat)
Trollius europaeus (See Globe-Flower)
Tropaeolum (See Nasturtium)

TRUMPET-VINE (*Campsis* or *Bignonia radicans*)

Lasts 3 to 4 days. Pick when 1 or 2 flowers are open in a cluster. Split woody stems. Condition overnight with stems in cold water. Some buds will drop off, but a good number will adhere long enough to open. Submerge foliage in cold water until firm and crisp, about ½ to 1 hour. Then split stems and keep in cold water till used.

TUBEROSE (*Polianthes tuberosa*)

Lasts 7 to 12 days. Cut when spikes are half to three-quarters open, but *before* the flowers on lower stem that open first begin to fade. Split stems. Condition overnight with stems in cold water reaching almost to flower-heads. Well-developed buds open in water; very tight buds do not. Remove faded flowers as upper buds open. Recut stems as necessary. Often flower-heads of tall varieties are too heavy to be supported by stems. Dwarf varieties have thick, short stems, which afford greater support.

TULIPS (*Tulipa* in variety)

Last 5 to 8 days. Tulips always turn their faces toward the light after they have been cut and arranged. Fully-developed buds open quickly. Cut Tulips in advanced-bud stage—when petals are about as long as they will be when flowers have opened. Cut off, or up through, the white portion at base of stems. Condition Tulips (a dozen or so together) by wrapping in wet newspaper and placing them in straight, tall containers of cold water reaching almost to flower-heads. (Newspaper should extend down into the water so it will remain wet. If not, it will dry and draw moisture from flowers.) Buds may be close together and touch when wrapped. This helps to prevent their opening. (See Plate 7.) Tulips, cut

Plate 7

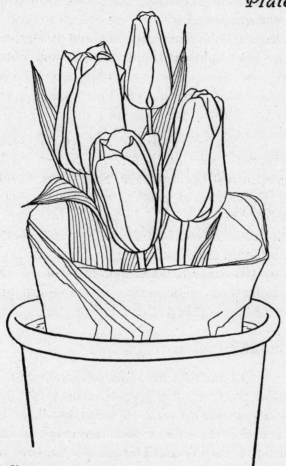

Conditioning tulips
    to prevent
    drooping
    of flower-heads

and conditioned overnight in this manner, are less likely to droop when arranged.

When exhibiting Tulips, drop slightly-cooled, melted candle wax into the cup where petals are joined. The wax, preferably the same color as the Tulips, will keep petals from unfolding and dropping off. For precise placement in arrangements, insert a florist's wire through each stem until it reaches the bottom of the flower, or run the wire through the base of the cup for a short way into the upper part of the stem. Have both Tulips and hands wet; it is a tricky operation. So wired, Tulips may be turned in any direction. (Little can be done with weak-stemmed Tulips except to use them in low arrangements.)

Turban Buttercup (See Ranunculus)
Turban Lily (See Lily, Turks-Cap)
Typha latifolia (See Cat-tail)
Valeriana officinalis (See Garden Heliotrope)

VEGETABLES

Vegetables like broccoli, cabbage, kale, okra, radishes, rhubarb, string beans, turnips, and others used in arrangements in warm rooms soon give off their characteristic odors. To check these, submerge vegetables in ice water for 1 to 2 hours. This also gives them a fresh, crisp appearance, and of course, makes them last longer. Wilted vegetables—purple or small green cabbages—can be shaped into new forms while in a pliable stage. You can make a small purple cabbage, for instance, look like a large rose. After shaping, submerge in ice water until leaves are crisp again.

VERBENA (*Verbena hortensis* or *V. hybrida*)

Lasts 5 to 7 days. Cut flowers when 2 or 3 outside rows of buds are completely open or when most buds are showing true color. Split stems ½ to 1 inch. Condition overnight with stems in warm water to which 1 teaspoon of sugar has been added for each quart.

Veronica (See Speedwell)
Vinca minor, V. major (See Periwinkle)
Vinca rosea (See Periwinkle, Madagascar)
Viola (See Pansy)
Viola odorata (See Violets)

VIOLETS (*Viola odorata*)

Last 4 to 7 days. Pick when fully opened. Buds do not open in water. Immediately submerge blooms in a large container of cold water for 1 hour. They will float to the top; gently push them down with the palm of your hand so that all flowers become soaking wet. When they are crisp and turgid, remove gently, shake free of excess water, and place with stems in cold water. Condition overnight before arranging.

If florist's Violets appear wilted, wrap stems in wax paper, to protect from the heat of your hand, and hold the bunch of flower-heads in cold water for several minutes, or until they appear fresh and crisp. Then recut stems and place in cold water until used. To capture their delicate fragrance, wrap violet bouquets loosely with wax paper. (See also Pansy, How to Keep Corsages.)

VIRGINIA BLUEBELL (*Mertensia virginica*)

Lasts 4 to 6 days. Cut when 3 or 4 of the nodding blossoms in each cluster are fully open. Remove leaves from lower stem. Split stems. Immediately place in hot water, 80° to 100° F., and let remain overnight. If flowers appear wilted after first placement of stems in hot water, remove them when it has cooled and place again in hot water. Two applications of hot water should always suffice to bring flowers to perfection for arranging.

Viscum flavescens (See Mistletoe)
Vitex Agnus-castus (See Chaste-Tree)

WALLFLOWER (*Cheiranthus Cheiri*)

Lasts 6 to 12 days. Cut when slightly less than half the cluster is open. Split stems which are sometimes woody. Condition overnight with stems in warm water to start with. Tall stems curve slightly when placed slantwise in the conditioning container.

WATERLILY (*Nymphaeaceae*)

Lasts 1 to 4 days. As you cut each flower, plunge stem at once into water. We turn to the Japanese for instructions in caring for cut Waterlilies, Lotus, and other water- or land-plants of similar stem-structure. Because of the honey-combed nature of the stems, when cut they fill up with air, and water cannot go up the stem. To circumvent this, the Japanese use a little pump which pulls air out and draws water in. Here these small pumps are not widely used; cutting stems under water approximates the results. Let the water in which stems are to be recut stand 10 minutes or so after drawing so air bubbles can escape. Otherwise, they will attach themselves to the bottom of the cut stems, defeating your purpose.

After recutting stems, let Waterlilies and Lotus remain in the same water at least 3 hours before arranging. Buds will open quickly if the conditioning container is placed in sunlight. After flowers are arranged, change water often, and, if you are using a shallow bowl, be sure to replenish water as it evaporates, and put a little alum in the water. (It has antiseptic value.) To force blossoms to stay open, drop melted wax—preferably of the same color as the flowers—inside the cup and around the base of the petals where they join in the center.

Tropical Waterlilies will offer you color around the clock if you grow day-bloomers, which are open from sunrise to sunset, and night-bloomers, which open early in the evening and close in the morning. Know the characteristics of your Waterlilies and use them to advantage as you strive for long-lasting flowers.

WHEAT (*Triticum aestivum*)

Why not grow a small quantity of wheat in your cutting garden to harvest when light-green, tan, or ripe for fresh or dried arrangements? Condition green wheat with stems in cold water overnight. It ripens somewhat after picking, holds its color and shape well. If stems are strong enough, dry upright in a basket or container without water. If stems are weak, and they usually are when green, hang upside-down in a dark, dry room. Watch out for mice where wheat is stored.

Wild Sweet William (See Phlox)
Wind-Flower (See Anemone)

WISHBONE-FLOWER (*Torenia Fournieri*)

Lasts 4 to 7 days. Lift entire plants when half in flower. They last well this way. Trim away excess foliage and the smallest buds. Wash soil from roots. Condition overnight with roots in cold water. If you cut flowers, select those fully open or nearly so, and condition the same way.

WISTERIA (*Wisteria* in variety)

Lasts 4 to 7 days. The whole cluster of the Chinese Wisteria bursts into bloom at once before leaves appear. Cut this type in the advanced-bud stage. The Japanese Wisteria (*W. Floribunda*) starts opening at the top of the long drooping cluster. The lower buds open slowly as the foliage leafs out. Cut this type when racemes are about one-quarter open, but always before the first florets begin to fade. Split woody stems of all Wisterias. Condition with stems in cold water overnight. Adjust water to pH 4 for best results (page 24). Spray blossoms and buds with a fine mist of cold water to prevent loss of moisture through petals. This also encourages buds to open.

Wolfbane (See Monkshood)

WOOLLY LAMBS-EAR (*Stachys lanata*)

Foliage is the attraction here. Cut any time after leaves have attained size you desire. Split stems. Condition overnight in warm water to start with. Flowers are not showy, but if you want them, cut when spikes are beginning to open and condition the same as the foliage.

Woolly Speedwell (See Speedwell)
Wormwood (See Artemesia)

YARROW OR MILFOIL (*Achillea* in variety)

Lasts 3 to 15 days, depending on variety. The 5-foot, yellow *filipendulina* lasts longest. Cut all of them when slightly over half the flowers in a cluster are open. Condition overnight with stems in cold water to which 2 tablespoons of salt has been added for each quart of water. Also dries well. Cut when flowers are fully open.

YORKTOWN ONION (*Allium ampeloprasum*)

Lasts 4 to 7 days. For use with fresh materials, cut when one-fourth to one-half the cluster is open. Recut stems just before placing in cold water to condition overnight. Place slantwise in a large container if you want curving stems. For drying, cut flowers when they are about three-fourths open. Tie in small bunches, and hang in the usual manner; *A. neapolitanum* is excellent to cut.

Yucca filamentosa (See Adams-Needle)
Zantedeschia in variety (See Lily, Calla)

ZINNIA (*Zinnia elegans*)

Lasts 1 to 2 weeks, slightly longer during cool weather. Cut when moisture-content is high after deep soaking of soil if weather is dry. Flowers should be completely open, but centers still tight. Buds do not open well after being cut. Remove lower leaves and as many others as you can spare. By almost complete defoliation, life is somewhat prolonged. Lose no time in plunging stems into cold water to condition overnight, or for at least 8 hours. With Z. *mexicana*, treat and condition as above, but put stems in warm water at the start.

IV

Drying, Pressing, Dyeing, Forcing, and Making Potpourri

~~~~~~~~~~~~~~~~~~~~~~~~~~~~~~~~~~~~~~~

HOW TO DRY FLOWERS

You WILL be delighted with results if you follow these suggestions:

Gather most flowers for drying at their peak of perfection, that is, just before they have fully opened. Between this stage and the time they are picked for drying, protect them from rain, wind, insects, and sprays.

Cut these in the advanced bud-stage, that is, *before* they are fully open: Everlastings (*Acroclinium* sp., *Helipterum* sp., and *Rhodanthe* sp.), Pearly Everlasting (*Anaphalis margaritacea*), Joe-Pye Weed (*Eupatorium maculatum, E. purpureum*), and Strawflowers (*Helichrysum bracteatum* and *H. Monstrosum*). The term, Everlasting, seems to be applied to all flowers which readily retain form and color after being dried.

Flowers shatter when dried if they are picked after their prime. If picked too early, they will not develop properly, nor retain shape or color. Experience alone will guide you in determining the proper stage for picking. It is not always easy to know the most perfect stage if you have not watched the same varieties growing year after year. Don't be discouraged if your first trial is not completely successful. Your second or third will be. If some flowers do shatter, check by spraying with clear plastic.

Before flowers have a chance to wilt (and this is very important) strip foliage from stems, and tie in small bunches, 12 to 16 each, depending on size of stems and of flower-heads. (Be sure no insects or worms are included.)

Hang bunches with flower-heads down in a dark, dry room. If the room is light, colors will fade. If it is damp, flowers will mildew. Should flowers wilt badly before you get around to bunching and hanging them, place stems in cold water until they become fresh and turgid. Then hang as described above.

When materials are well dried—and I find it usually takes longer than the recommended 2 to 3 weeks—store in roomy boxes or dust-free containers until you are ready to use them.

With grains, Globe Amaranth, and Clover, watch out for mice.

If such sturdy material as Okra and Artichoke is too stiff and straight for arranging when dried, make it pliable by holding stems over steam from a teakettle. You can then bend them into pleasing curves. Allow to dry in the new positions before placing in your arrangement.

An amazing number of flowers and foliage-plants dry well, retaining their natural forms and brilliant colors. Some that seem to have no possibilities, such as Perillia foliage and leaves of Hostas, after hanging several weeks in a dark room delight us with their forms and colors. Try everything and anything that looks as if it had the slightest potential, and even things that don't! And sometimes, for a change, introduce green or fresh plant material to your dried arrangements. It will make them more interesting.

Fill containers for dried arrangements with moist sand or vermiculite. When either dries, it seems to hold stems more securely than if you start out with it dry. No further moistening is necessary.

After your arrangement is completed, if the container has a wide enough opening, pour melted wax over the dried-out sand and in between the flower-stems. Solidified wax holds an arrangement perfectly and permanently in position.

If dried stems are *very* stiff, or have been fastened to picks, you can insert them directly in floral clay and color this so as to conceal it when using with driftwood or in shallow containers. Work instant coffee into clay to color it tan or brown. Use green, gray or other colored modeling clay to match container or arrangement.

Dip stem-ends of dried materials in warm wax. This increases the size and makes them adhere more securely to pinholders.

GLYCERIN-AND-WATER TREATMENT FOR FOLIAGE

Treat branches of Magnolia, Beech, Dogwood, and Eucalyptus, also Lemon or Salal leaves, and other foliages, with a glycerin solution to make them last well and color attractively.

Select well-defined branches, curved or straight. Look for healthy foliage, not torn or defaced.

Trim leaves and side branches away from base of main stems. Split these for 2 to 3 inches. If there is any dust or spray residue, wash or spray leaves with cold water to cleanse them.

Prepare a solution of 1 part glycerin (from the drugstore) and 2 parts water.

Place stems in container so at least 6 inches extend into the solution. As branches take it up, leaves turn golden, dark-brown, or bronze, the color depending on the type of foliage. Make certain there is enough solution in the container. Some branches absorb a large quantity in a short time. Recutting stems about once a week, removing ½ to 1 inch each time, hastens the absorption process. It takes 2 to 3 weeks, perhaps a little longer for thick leathery leaves. When desired color is attained, remove material from solution. Store in dust-free boxes or even a bureau drawer. No water is needed. Glycerin-treated foliage retains quality and color for years and may be used over and over again.

With Galax leaves and English Ivy, submerge completely in a half-and-half solution of glycerin and water. Late spring until midsummer is the best time to treat these two. At this time they absorb the solution more readily.

Material treated with glycerin and water may be arranged dry or combined with fresh flowers since water will not injure treated stems.

BORAX METHOD

The borax method is excellent for preserving delicate flowers which are not adaptable to drying by hanging—Clematis, Cosmos, Daffodils, Gladiolus, single and double Hibiscus, Lilies, and Peonies. Flowers should be freshly picked, stripped of foliage, and placed, heads down, in a box containing an inch of powdered borax or a mixture of half and half fine dry sand and borax, well mixed. Sift more borax, or borax and sand, gently through and around petals until each bloom is completely covered.

Lay flowers like Daffodils, Lilacs, and Snapdragons lengthwise in a box, and cover the same way. When removing flowers from box, handle very carefully to prevent crumbling.

Varying lengths of time are required for drying. Light-textured flowers, Babys-Breath and Daffodils, require only 1 to 2 days. Marigolds and Zinnias may need 4 to 5, or longer. Flowers with thick petals and much moisture, like Camellias and Magnolias, require more time than those with thin, fragile petals like Forget-Me-Nots.

The color of most flowers fades to some extent, although Roses and Zinnias retain their hues remarkably well. Picking at just the right time helps.

Use moth balls and a sprinkling of borax in the storage boxes to protect flowers and foliages from carpet beetles and other insects.

HOW TO PRESS LEAVES, FERNS, FLOWERS

Pressing is an ancient method of preserving leaves, ferns, and flowers. Gather material to be pressed in as nearly perfect condition as you can find it. Trim side shoots or branches so none overlaps. Brush leaves lightly with a non-salty oil like olive oil.

Before material has a chance to wilt, place each piece between several thicknesses of dry newspaper. Build up a pile, keeping it as level as possible.

Weight down with a large flat board, with another weight on top; bricks or heavy books will do.

Allow 3 to 12 weeks for drying, depending on climate

and humidity. When material is completely dried, remove from between newspapers; store in dry, dust-free containers. (If left between newspapers too long, moisture that has been absorbed by the paper will seep back into the foliage, spoiling it.) For more extensive information on dried material, see *The Complete Book of Dried Arrangements* by Raye Miller Underwood (M. Barrows & Co., Inc., New York).

HERE IS A LIST OF GOOD PLANTS TO DRY:

Acroclinium (Also known as *Helipterum*). Pick in advanced-bud stage. Hang.

Ageratum, Annual (*Ageratum Houstinanum*). Cut fully open. Hang. Perennial (*Eupatorium coelestinum*). Cut fully open. Hang.

Amaranth (*Gomphrena globosa*). Cut three-quarters to fully open. Hang.

Artemesia, Silver King and Silver Queen. Cut when fully open. Also cut and hang foliage. Hang or Borax Method.

Artemesia (*Artemesia lactiflora*). Cut when fully open. Also cut and hang foliage. Hang or Borax Method.

Baptisia (*Baptisia australis*). Treat seed pods and foliage with glycerin and water.

Bayberry (*Myrica caroliniensis*). Gather when berries are formed. Treat foliage in glycerin and water.

Bee-Balm (*Monarda didyma*). Cut when three-quarters open. Hang.

Bittersweet (*Celastrus scandens*). Gather fruits when ripe *before* heavy frosts and rains. Hang.

Butterfly Weed (*Asclepias tuberosa*). Cut when fully open. Hang.

Cat-tail (*Typha latifolia*). Pick before shattering starts. Spray with clear plastic if necessary. Store in upright container.

Clover (*Trifolium*). Cut when three-quarters open. Hang.

Cockscomb (*Celosia*). Cut when at most beautiful stage. Hang.

Cones and Pods of Arborvitae, Cedar, Cryptomeria, Hemlock, Pine. Gather at any time except in freezing or very dry weather.

Corn: Foliage, Tassels, Ears. Paint dried foliage gold or silver. Pull back husks of corn ears before drying. Hang tassels.

Cupid's Dart (*Catananche coerulea*). Cut fully open. Hang.

Dock (*Rumex*). Pick at various stages of green, tan, and brown. Hang.

Golden Ageratum (*Lonas inodora*). Cut when three-quarters open. Hang.

Goldenrod (*Solidago canadensis*). Cut fully open. Hang or Borax Method.

Gourds. Shellac or paint. Collect when leaves of vine wither naturally and gourd shells are very hard. Store in cold place after cleansing in solution of Sylpho Napthol, using 1 teaspoon to each quart of water.

Grains. Rye, Millet, Barley, Wheat, Oats. Collect in two or three stages, green to tan. Hang.

Grasses. Collect in early and advanced stages. Hang.

Honesty or Penny-Flower (*Lunaria biennis*). Collect seed pods when they are turning tan. Hang. Remove outer covering when completely dried.

House Plants. Any large leaves with substance. Hang or experiment with Borax Method.

Immortelle (*Xeranthemum annuum*). Difficult to grow, but one of the best and most attractive dried flowers. Cut when fully open. Hang.

Jobs-Tears (*Coix lachrymae*). Cut when some seeds are black, some tan, some light-green. Hang.

Joe-Pye Weed (*Eupatorium purpureum*). Pick in bud. Hang.

Kale Flowers. When fully open. Hang or Borax Method.

Knotweed (*Polygonum*). Gather when pink fruits are formed. Hang or place in upright containers.

Larkspur (*Delphinium ajacis*). Cut when three-quarters open. Hang, or Borax Method.

Leaves. Beech, Dogwood, Hickory, Maple, Oak, Sassafras. Cut when fall colors are at their height. Press. Beech, Magnolia and others may also be treated in glycerin and water.

Marigold (*Tagetes erecta*). Cut when three-quarters open. Hang or Borax Method.

Okra Pods. Pick when green and of desired size. Select with interesting curves. Hang.

Pearl Everlasting (*Anaphalis margaritacea*). Pick in bud. Hang.

Queen-Annes-Lace (*Daucus carota*). Hang fruits. Press the open flowers.

Rhubarb Flowers. When fully open. Hang or Borax Method.

Rose Hips. When they are of good color. Hang.

Roses. Bright red or yellow varieties are best. Cut in advanced-bud stage. Hang. Also use Borax Method on some partially opened blooms.

Sage (*Salvia farinacea*). When three-quarters open. Hang.

Sand-Flower (See Winged Everlasting)

Scotch Broom (*Sytisus scoparius*). Green branches. Dry or press, or treat with glycerin and water.

Sea-Lavender (*Limonium latifolium*). When three-quarters open. Hang.

Seed Pods. Especially of Blackberry-Lily, Gas-Plant, Iris, Lilies, Snakeroot, Thalictrum, Thermopsis, Tree Peony, Unicorn and Yucca. Gather when ripe and at most beautiful stage. Hang.

Spirea (*Astilbe*). Gather at its prime. Hang.

Statice or Sea-Lavender (*Limonium*). Cut when fully open. Hang.

Stock (*Mathiola incana*). Cut before florets on base of stalk begin to fade. Hang, or use Borax Method.

Strawflower (*Helichrysum*). Cut in bud. Hang.

Sumac (*Rhus*). Cut when fruits are brilliant. Hang or store in upright containers.

Tansy (*Tanacetum vulgare*). When fully open. Hang.

Thistle (*Cirsium*). When about three-quarters open. Hang.

Vines and tendrils of Clematis, Wisteria, etc. Hang.

Winged Everlasting (*Ammobium alatum*). When fully open. Hang.

Yarrow (*Achillea mullifolium*). When fully open. Hang.

Zinnia (*Zinnia elegans*). When fully open. Hang, or use Borax Method.

HOW TO DYE FLOWERS

White flowers can be dyed many lovely colors with food coloring, writing inks (especially red), show-card Tempera Color (for dipping Calla Lilies only), or dyes made especially for flowers (Floradye).

You can either dip the flower-heads, fresh or dried, into

a colored solution; or place the cut stems of fresh flowers in a solution and let stems draw color up into the blooms. To hasten the dyeing, recut stems *under* the dye solution, and to get a nice, even shade through all the petals, leave flowers out of water for some time before placing stems in a solution. The time varies according to the nature of the flower being dyed. For Gladiolus and Carnations, 2 to 3 hours is sufficient. Less sturdy flowers that show signs of wilting or softness are ready to go into the dye solution sooner. After the desired color is reached, take stems from dye and make your arrangement, or keep stems in water in a dim room until used. Bright light sometimes makes dyed flowers fade, so it is best to dye them reasonably close to the time they will be used.

HOW TO MAKE DYES

Mix vegetable food coloring with water until you get the color you want.

Use show-card Tempera Color for dipping Calla Lilies. Mix 1 tablespoon of color thinned down with 1 to 2 quarts of warm water, depending on depth of color desired. Wait to dip Callas until solution has cooled. Then place stems in water until used.

For dipping fresh or dried flowers and for dyeing fresh flowers through the stems, use Floradye as directed on container, or make dyes with ink as follows: Use a 10-cent bottle of ink (¾ to 1-ounce size) and 4 teaspoons of powdered alum in each pint of water. (Preferably use rain- or well-water, especially in July and August, to avoid the chemicals in city water.)

Here Are Some Color Suggestions:

Blue-Green—Use Parker Green Ink or Waterman Tropic Green Ink.

Flag-Blue—Use Parker Permanent Blue-Black Ink and Parker Royal-Blue Ink, mixed half and half.

Medium-Blue—Use Parker or Waterman Permanent Blue Ink.

Salmon-Pink—Use Sanford Cardinal-Red Ink. (Different shades of yellow Chrysanthemums or other yellow flowers dipped into this solution produce Peach, Apricot, and Orange shades.)

Deep-Pink—Use Sanford or Higgins Red Stamp-Pad Ink. (2-ounce bottle will make 1 quart; use 8 teaspoons of powdered alum with this amount.)

Experiment with other colors as you wish.

FORCING FLOWERING BRANCHES

Best results are obtained when materials to be forced are cut after buds begin to swell in late winter and early spring. If cut too early, buds shrivel, fail to mature, or drop off before opening. When cut too late, plants are likely to blossom outdoors before branches open indoors, so nothing is gained.

Before cutting, consider the natural blooming time of shrub or tree. A good time to cut is about 6 to 8 weeks ahead of normal flowering. You can cut earlier, but flowers will not be so good. Cut so as to prune judiciously. Select good-sized branches with pleasing curves and angles to suit the arrangement you have in mind.

Split stems 3 to 4 inches. Place stems in large containers of cold water in a room temperature of 65° to 70° F. Put a few pieces of charcoal in the water to keep it sweet, and change the water at least weekly. You can use the same charcoal again. Each time you change the water, cut off about 1 inch of the stem. Spray with a fine mist of cold water daily, or at least twice a week for added humidity and as encouragement to buds to open. This has the same effect as rain.

A semishady section of a greenhouse or the shadiest part of a sunroom is ideal for forcing; otherwise, a light, but not very sunny, window. Filtered sunlight is best. Strong, direct sun dries out the buds. As blossoms open, branches may be moved into bright sunshine to intensify colors. If there is too little sun available, colors will not be true. To obtain various shades for an arrangement, move some branches to full sun; as these open, keep others in shade.

If you want flowering branches for a certain date and their stage of development indicates they may be late in opening, you can speed things up by placing stems in hot water, 100° F. Do this once a day, letting branches remain until water cools. If branches seem too far advanced for the desired time, move them to a cool, dim room to retard opening of buds.

Bibliography

Bolton, Eleanor. *'Til Summer Comes Again*. Printed by the author, at Fairfax, Va., 1954.

Fry, J. M. *Care of Cut Flowers for Home Use*. Bulletin. Division of Agriculture Extension, College of Agriculture, The Pennsylvania State College, State College, Pa.

Gannon, Ruth. *Winter Bouquets With Color*. New York: Studio Publications, 1949.

Herbaceous Perennials. Bulletin 1381, U. S. Department of Agriculture. Washington, D. C.: Government Printing Office.

Kamp, J. R. and Pokorny, F. A. *Keeping Cut Flowers, A Preliminary Report*. Bulletin 146, Nov.-Dec., 1952. Illinois State Florists' Association, Urbana, Ill.

Kamp, J. R. *More About Cut Flowers*. Bulletin 148, March-April, 1953. Illinois State Florists' Association, Urbana, Ill.

———. "The Importance of Acidity (pH) in Keeping of Cut Flowers." *Flower Growing No. 3* (Bulletin). Extension Service in Agriculture and Home Economics, College of Agriculture, University of Illinois, Urbana.

Kemp, May D. *Flower Arrangement*. Circular 307. Division of Agriculture Extension, College of Agriculture, The Pennsylvania State College, State College, Pa.

Leyel, Mrs. C. F. *Magic of Herbs*. London: Jonathan Cape, 1926.

Marcus, Margaret Fairbanks. *Period Flower Arrangement*. New York: M. Barrows & Company, 1952.

Nishikawa, Issotei. *Floral Art of Japan*. Tokyo: Japan Travel Bureau, 1952.

Post, Kenneth and Fischer, C. W., Jr. *Commercial Storage of Cut Flowers*. Cornell Extension Bulletin 853, January, 1952. Cornell University, Ithaca, N. Y.

Ries, Victor H. *How to Keep Cut Flowers*. Bulletin. Extension Service, Ohio State University, Columbus, Ohio.

Tincker, M. A. H. "The Care of Cut Flowers," *Journal of the Royal Horticultural Society*, Part I, 67 (11): 373-380; Part II, 67 (12): 392-395.

Underwood, Raye Miller. *The Complete Book of Dried Arrangements*. New York: M. Barrows & Company, 1952.

Whitlock, Sarah and Rankin, Martha. *Drying Flowers for Color*. Printed by the author, at Charlottesville, Va., 1954.

Wood, Anne Wertsner. *The Flower-Show Guide*. New York: M. Barrows & Company, 1954.

Wood, Mary Cokely. *Flower Arrangement Art of Japan*. Rutland, Vt.: Charles E. Tuttle Company, 1951.

Index